AIR CAMPAIGN

NORWAY 1940

The Luftwaffe's Scandinavian Blitzkrieg

JAMES S. CORUM | ILLUSTRATED BY GRAHAM TURNER

OSPREY PUBLISHING
Bloomsbury Publishing Plc
PO Box 883, Oxford, OX1 9PL, UK
29 Earlsfort Terrace, Dublin 2, Ireland
1385 Broadway, 5th Floor, New York, NY 10018, USA
E-mail: info@ospreypublishing.com
www.ospreypublishing.com

OSPREY is a trademark of Osprey Publishing Ltd

First published in Great Britain in 2021

ISBN: PB 9781472847454; eBook 9781472847447;
ePDF 9781472847423; XML 9781472847430

21 22 23 24 25   10 9 8 7 6 5 4 3 2 1
Maps by www.bounford.com
Diagrams by Adam Tooby
3D BEVs by Paul Kime
Index by Zoe Ross
Typeset by PDQ Digital Media Solutions, Bungay, UK
Printed and bound in India by Replika Press Private Ltd.

Osprey Publishing supports the Woodland Trust, the UK's leading woodland conservation
charity.
To find out more about our authors and books visit www.ospreypublishing.com. Here
you will find extracts, author interviews, details of forthcoming events and the option to
sign up for our newsletter.

Glossary
Fallschirmjäger: Paratroopers
Fliegerkorps: Air Corps
Gebirgs-Division: Mountain Division
Jagdgeschwader (JG): Fighter Wing
Kampfgeschwader (KG): Bomber Wing
Kampfgeschwader (KG zbV): Special Purpose Transport Wing (*Kampfgeschwader*, literally
translated as 'Bomber Wing'. However, in 1940 a 'Special Purpose' (zbV) bomber wing
specified a transport wing. Later these wings would be called 'Transport Geschwader'.)
Kampfgruppe (KGr): Bomber Group
Kampfgruppe (KGr zbV): Special Purpose Transport Group (KGr zbV denoted a transport,
not bomber, group)
Kriegsmarine: German Navy
Küstenfliegergruppe (Kü Fl Gr): Coastal Aviation Group
Lehrgeschwader (LG): Training Wing
Luftflotte: Air Fleet
Sturzkampfgeschwader (StG): Stuka (dive bomber) Wing
Zerstörergeschwader (ZG): Heavy Fighter Wing

CONTENTS

INTRODUCTION

Ju 88 medium bomber. The Ju 88 entered Luftwaffe service in 1939. With a top speed of 292mph, a range of 1,800km and able to carry a 2,000kg bombload, the twin-engine medium bomber with a four-man crew became the Luftwaffe's main medium bomber for most of the war. It was a rugged aircraft, capable of dive bombing, and handled well. It was a highly versatile platform that was adapted as a very successful night fighter and long-range reconnaissance aircraft. Germany built more than 15,000 Ju 88s in many variants.
(Author's collection)

Admiral Erich Raeder, Commander-in-Chief of the German Navy. Raeder was the main proponent of Germany's invasion of Norway and convinced Hitler to authorize a campaign that would employ the Kriegsmarine's entire surface fleet.
(Author's collection)

The German Navy, or Kriegsmarine, was the primary driver of the campaign to seize and occupy Norway. One of the main lessons that the Kriegsmarine had learned from World War I was the ability of Britain's Royal Navy to carry out a highly damaging naval blockade of Germany. In 1929 Admiral Wegener, one of Germany's leading naval strategists, wrote a book, *Die Seestrategie des Weltkrieges* (*The Naval Strategy of the World War*), that argued that Norway held the pivotal strategic position for the German Navy. His view was that if the Germans had occupied Norway during the war, the British blockade would have been outflanked and Germany could have used Norwegian ports such as Trondheim to give its U-boats access to the North Atlantic. Wegener's book was read widely within the naval officer corps and was influential on German naval thinking. There were other factors that made Norway important. A large part of the Swedish iron ore required by German industry was shipped through Norway from the ice-free northern port of Narvik. Keeping Swedish iron-ore shipments secure was important to the Wehrmacht. Finally, Norway was important to secure the German flank if war came with Britain. If Norway were occupied by British forces, then Norwegian airbases could be used by RAF bombers to attack northern Germany.

When Germany went to war with Britain, the Kriegsmarine began thinking of occupying Norway. On 9 October 1939 Admiral Dönitz, commander of the U-boats, sent a memo to the operations staff of the navy arguing that the harbour of Trondheim, in Norway's central west coast, would be an ideal location for a U-boat base. In October and November, the Kriegsmarine's commander, Admiral Raeder, passed

on to Hitler the memo about the use of Norway by U-boats and met with Hitler in early December to urge the occupation of the Norwegian coast. A few days later, a secret visit to Berlin in December 1939 by Vidkun Quisling, a former Norwegian war minister and the leader of Norway's Nasjonal Samling Party, a minuscule pro-Nazi party, brought Norway's position to Hitler's attention. Quisling favoured an alliance with Germany and met with Nazi leaders and Admiral Raeder. Raeder and Nazi leaders arranged for Quisling to meet with Hitler on 14 December 1939. While Hitler made no promises to Quisling, the idea of occupying Norway appealed to him. With the Polish campaign over and the campaign in the West in the planning stages, Hitler had a lull in which to consider a major strategic move. On 19 December Hitler directed OKW (Oberkommando der Wehrmacht) to make a staff study of the possibility of invading Norway. A small staff was created called 'Studie Nord' and directed to report to OKW on the feasibility of an invasion of Norway.

CHRONOLOGY

1939
10 October Admiral Raeder, Commander-in-Chief, Kriegsmarine, meets with Hitler and reminds Hitler of the danger to Germany if the British occupy Norway.

November The United Kingdom Ministry of Economic Warfare sends a report to the cabinet that iron-ore traffic to Germany through Norway has been vastly increased.

11 December Vidkun Quisling, Nazi-sympathizing Norwegian politician and former war minister, visits Berlin and meets with Admiral Raeder.

14 December Raeder arranges for Quisling to meet with Hitler and Quisling discusses bringing Norway into the Nazi orbit.

16 December Churchill, First Lord of the Admiralty, submits a memo to the British Cabinet advocating the mining of Norwegian waters.

18 December The British chiefs of staff submit a report to the Cabinet recommending that a force be prepared to intervene in Norway.

19 December A German staff study on the invasion and occupation of Norway, 'Studie Nord', begins.

January 1940
January Out of 'Studie Nord', a special planning staff is organized under the navy's Captain Theodor Kranke.

2 January The British chiefs of staff recommend a much larger force for military intervention in Norway.

6 January The British War Office directs that some units be held in readiness to be deployed to Scandinavia – mainly Norway, but possibly Sweden.

19 January The British military begins planning for the Norway intervention, codenamed 'Avonmouth'. Planning is based on providing a force of 80,000 men and 10,000 vehicles under a corps headquarters. It should be ready by April. Air support in the form of two bomber squadrons, two fighter squadrons, and one army cooperation flight is envisioned.

27 January German planners assign the codename *Weserübung* to the operation.

February 1940
5 February The Allied Supreme War Council meets in France. The French agree to provide units for an expeditionary force to Norway.

5 February Using assistance to Finland as a rationale, the Allied Supreme War Council decides on intervention in Norway. Initial plans are for a landing at Narvik, and success would rely on the acquiescence of Norway and Sweden. Despite the stated rationale, cutting supplies of iron ore to Germany is a prime motivation for the plan.

16 February The British destroyer HMS *Cossack* intercepts the German transport *Altmark* in Norwegian waters, recovering 299 British prisoners of war. The *Altmark* incident makes public the Allies' readiness to intervene in Norway and provides impetus to German planners to accelerate their plans.

The incident that started it all: the German prison ship *Altmark*, cornered and taken by the British destroyer HMS *Cossack* in Jøssingfjord. In February, the Royal Navy freed 300 British prisoners from the *Altmark*, thus alerting the Germans that the British would not allow them to misuse Norwegian territorial waters and that they were ready to carry out naval action to stop any German intentions on Norway. (Popperfoto via Getty Images)

21 February General Nikolaus von Falkenhorst is appointed to command the invasion of Norway.

March 1940
1 March A final order is given for the German attack on Norway and Denmark.

3 March The German date for invasion is set for 17 March 1940; this is later delayed to April.

28 March The Allies decide to begin mining Norwegian waters (Operation *Wilfred*), and to send a military force to Norway to pre-empt German moves. Mining operations are set to start on 5 April, but this is moved back to 8 April.

April 1940
1 April Hitler approves final plans for the attacks on Norway and Denmark.

2 April Germany sets 9 April 1940 as the date for *Weserübung*.

3 April Winston Churchill becomes the chair of the British Ministerial Defence Committee. One of his first actions is to get consent for mining operations in Norwegian territorial waters.

5 April France and the United Kingdom notify Norway of their reservation of the right to deny Germany access to Norwegian resources.

6 April British Admiralty receives a report from Copenhagen stating ten German destroyers are headed towards Narvik but considers the possibility of such an event doubtful.

7 April German vessels begin to set to sea for Operation *Weserübung*; some are seen by RAF reconnaissance. Home Fleet moves north northeast in search of the enemy; it is joined by the 2nd Cruiser Squadron. Home Fleet remains well to the west of the Norwegian coast, Admiral Forbes believing that the German heavy ships are attempting a commerce-raiding breakout into the Atlantic. The German invasion groups, on their way to Norwegian ports, stay close to the coast and are not intercepted by the Royal Navy.

8 April HMS *Glowworm* is sunk by the German heavy cruiser *Admiral Hipper* off the Norwegian coast. The Polish submarine ORP *Orzeł* sinks the German transport *Rio de Janeiro* at the southern Norwegian coast. The government in Oslo is informed and alerts are issued to the coastal defence and airfields, but the government refrains from calling for an immediate mobilization.

9 April Denmark is overrun and surrenders in one morning. Successful German paratroop landings seize Aalborg airfield and key bridges connecting Zealand.

Blücher is sunk by shore batteries along Oslo Fjord and naval/land attack on Oslo delayed. German air-landed soldiers capture the airport at Oslo. Air-landed soldiers

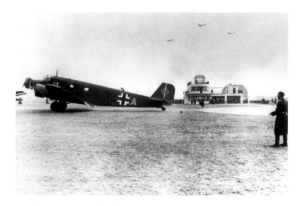

Ju 52 transports at Aalborg, Denmark, on 10 April. Aalborg, a modern airfield with a concrete runway, served as a staging and refuelling point for German aircraft flying into Norway. It would be one of the main German airfields for *Weserübung* with bomber, fighter and patrol units stationed there to cover the North Sea. (ullstein bild via Getty Images)

march in and occupy Oslo with no resistance. Successful landings at Kristiansand and Bergen and Trondheim. The Narvik landing force lands 2,500 German mountain troops and takes the city.

Paratroop landings at Stavanger secure the airfield and a regiment flown in occupies the city. Stavanger becomes the key German airbase in Norway.

German naval task forces occupy Bergen, Narvik, Egersund and Kristiansand.

The Norwegian King and government flee Oslo in the morning and set up the seat of government 70km north at Hamar.

10 April The First Battle of Narvik occurs when a British force of five destroyers enters Ofotfjord. The British lose two ships; the Germans lose two of their ten destroyers, with three others badly damaged. The Royal Navy now controls the mouth of Narvik's fjord.

At Bergen, the German cruiser *Königsberg* is sunk by air attack by Fleet Air Arm Skuas flying from Hatston Naval Air Station.

In Oslo, Vidkun Quisling tries to set up a government and cabinet without approval of the King or legislature. The Norwegians, who might have negotiated an armistice, reject any diplomacy with the Germans.

General Laake is relieved as the Norwegian Army commander and Colonel Otto Ruge, now promoted to major general, is named army commander. Ruge is out of contact with most of his forces due to the poor communications capabilities of the Norwegian Army.

11 April Luftwaffe bombers bomb the town of Elverum.

12 April RAF Bomber Command sends 83 aircraft to attack German shipping at Stavanger without success, with nine bombers lost.

Fleet Air Arm bombers attack Bergen but fail to hit any German ships.

Germans stand up Luftflotte 5 as the higher-level Luftwaffe headquarters in Norway. Generaloberst Erhard Milch is named commander. X Fliegerkorps remains directing flying operations, while Luftflotte 5 takes charge of Luftwaffe logistics, airfield engineers, administrative units, and flak forces.

The Luftwaffe occupies Værnes airfield near Trondheim and finds it barely usable. Hundreds of local workers are hired to build a new hard runway. In the meantime, the Germans use a frozen lake just a few kilometres from Trondheim's centre as an airstrip.

13 April Thirteen Luftwaffe Ju 52s fly a mountain artillery battery to frozen Lake Hartvig near Narvik. The aircraft freeze onto the lake's icy surface and cannot be extricated. Twelve will be lost; one is able to fly off but lands in Sweden and is interned.

13–20 April Trondheim is reinforced to counter a likely British attack. Luftwaffe transports fly in 3,000 infantry, artillery and flak troops as well as some artillery and flak guns.

13 April The Second Battle of Narvik occurs when a British force of nine destroyers and the battleship HMS *Warspite* enter Ofotfjord and destroy all eight remaining German destroyers. Four destroyers beach themselves at Rombaksfjord, and the 1,900 surviving sailors are organized into naval infantry battalions. Generalleutnant Dietl holds Narvik with 4,400 men but is cut off from supplies by the Royal Navy. Only the occasional airdrop by long-range aircraft can sustain the force.

14 April British forces land at Namsos and Harstad as Anglo–French forces build up a base at Harstad for the campaign. Allied commanders link up with General Fleischer, commander of the Norwegian 6th Division in the far north. The 6th Division is the only Norwegian Army division at full strength and mobilized on 9 April. The 6th Division establishes a front line in the mountains 25km north of Narvik.

14 April German paratroopers make a combat jump at Dombås in poor weather. Paratroopers are scattered into small bands and are hunted down and forced to surrender over the next five days by Norwegian troops.

15 April Vidkun Quisling forced out of office by the Germans.

German forces, arriving by sea and air, move through southern Norway and occupy the populated areas with little Norwegian resistance.

The British 24th Brigade lands at Harstad at the mouth of Narvik's fjord. Harstad will become the main Allied base for the Narvik campaign.

16 April The British 146th Brigade lands at Namsos. This is the first unit of 'Mauriceforce', with a mission of encircling and cutting off the German garrison at Trondheim from the north. The brigade moves south to the key rail and road junction at Steinkjer, 70km north of Trondheim. The British link up with two understrength Norwegian battalions. Due to the problems of unloading at Namsos' small port, as well as poorly planned logistics, the British force lacks heavy weapons and support units.

Advance elements of the British 148th Brigade land at Åndalsnes south of Trondheim. The 148th Brigade is named 'Sickleforce' and has the mission of attacking Trondheim from the south. The Norwegians appeal for help in holding the entrance to the Gudbrandsdal Valley, so the British commander changes the mission and sends units of the 148th Brigade by rail to Lillehammer to link up with General Ruge's 2nd Division. The 148th Brigade lacks heavy weapons and supplies.

17 April British heavy cruiser HMS *Suffolk* bombards German-held Stavanger for one hour in the early

Reconnaissance photograph of Sola airfield, Stavanger, taken by the RAF on 17 April 1940. Despite repeated bombings and a naval bombardment by the Royal Navy cruiser HMS *Suffolk*, Stavanger remained in operation and suffered relatively little damage through the campaign. (© Imperial War Museums, C 1252)

morning. The main damage is to the seaplane base 1km from the main airfield. Sixty-plus Luftwaffe bomber sorties from Stavanger target HMS *Suffolk* in a four-hour running battle. The *Suffolk* is hit by two bombs and severely damaged. It arrives at Scapa Flow sinking. It will be out of action until February 1941.

18 April The British 148th Brigade main force lands at Åndalsnes. The French 5e Demi-Brigade de Chasseurs Alpins lands at Namsos.

A battle group of 2,500 troops is organized by the Germans at Trondheim to move against the British 148th Brigade at Steinkjer. The Germans are backed by a destroyer and torpedo boat and make landings on the British flank. The Germans have ample air support and naval gunfire support.

19 April The British 146th Brigade is forced to withdraw from Steinkjer by German forces.

20 April German air raids destroy Namsos and its harbour along with a large part of the supplies of the Allied force.

German forces moving north from Oslo reach Lillehammer and capture the town the next day.

21 April Hitler orders 2. Gebirgs-Division to be sent to Norway.

22 April German Gruppe Pellengahr attacks the British 148th Brigade north of Lillehammer. The British/Norwegian force retreats. Germans advance into Gudbrandsdal, the main rail and road route to Trondheim through central Norway.

Luftwaffe bombers attack Åndalsnes and Namsos, inflicting heavy damage on the Allied logistics.

23 April The British 15th Brigade lands at Åndalsnes and moves to relieve the 148th Brigade. It arrives too late and the 148th Brigade is broken by Gruppe Pellengahr, which has artillery and air support from Luftwaffe bombers.

24 April Gladiators of RAF No. 263 Squadron arrive via aircraft carrier *Glorious* at frozen Lake Lesjaskog southeast of Åndalsnes. They have the mission of supporting the Allied ground forces in Gudbrandsdal and providing air cover.

British carriers *Glorious* and *Ark Royal* take position 225km off the coast, and their aircraft fly cover for Sickleforce. British 15th Brigade deploys at Kvam to halt Gruppe Pellengahr advancing from Lillehammer. Remnants of 148th Brigade retreat to Kvam after losing half the brigade as prisoners and casualties.

Fleet Air Arm Swordfish from carrier *Ark Royal* attack Trondheim's Værnes airfield.

25 April German forces push back Allied forces in the Gudbrandsdal north of Lillehammer.

Norwegian forces attack the German defence line north of Narvik, but the German lines hold.

Three Royal Navy trawlers sunk by Luftwaffe attacks off Åndalsnes.

Heavy Luftwaffe attacks against RAF No. 263 Squadron at Lake Lesjaskog. The squadron's aircraft are destroyed on the ground.

French 27e Demi-Brigade de Chasseurs Alpins arrives at Harstad near Narvik.

28 April The British Cabinet decides on the evacuation of Allied forces from central Norway. A brigade of French mountain troops arrives at Harstad.

29 April King Haakon and the Norwegian government evacuate Molde and travel to Tromsø. German forces from Gruppe Fischer link up with the Trondheim force. Heavy German air attacks at Åndalsnes and Namsos. Royal Navy sloop *Bittern* sunk by Luftwaffe aircraft at Namsos.

30 April Allied evacuations begin at Åndalsnes.

May 1940

1 May Allies complete evacuation of 4,400 troops at Åndalsnes.

2 May German forces enter Åndalsnes. Mauriceforce evacuates 5,400 Allied troops at Namsos. Anglo-French forces land at Mosjøen to block German advances to Bodø.

3 May Mauriceforce evacuation is delayed by thick fog. Junkers Ju 87 dive bombers attack the convoy at sea and sink French destroyer *Bison* and British destroyer *Afridi* with heavy loss of life. Luftwaffe aircraft attack Allied shipping off Narvik.

Royal Navy cruiser taking evasive action from Luftwaffe bombs. The Luftwaffe found that, against rapidly moving ships, high-altitude bombing was very inaccurate. The most effective anti-ship bomber of the Luftwaffe was the Ju 87. Operating in pairs, Stukas could line up on either side of a targeted ship and effectively attack it either way it turned. (Author's collection)

4 May Polish destroyer *Grom* sunk by Luftwaffe aircraft off Narvik.

5 May French Foreign Legion brigade and a Polish brigade land at Harstad. German force composed mostly of 2. Gebirgs-Division troops under Lieutenant General Feuerstein begins ground advance towards Bodø starting from Grong, where the Germans establish a logistics base.

10 May German and Allied troops clash at Mosjøen as British forces are sent south to reinforce. Elements of German 2. Gebirgs-Division attack towards Mosjøen. General Hans-Jürgen Stumpff takes command of Luftflotte 5. General Milch returns to Berlin. Meanwhile, the great spring offensive of the Wehrmacht begins, with France and the Low Countries attacked by 120 German divisions.

13 May Norwegian forces begin the advance on Narvik from the northern flank. French carry out successful landing at Bjerkvik 10km north of Narvik and outflank the German defence line. Germans retreat to final defence line near Narvik.

14–27 May German force at Narvik reinforced by 600 paratroops landed in groups of 60–100 over two weeks. Some of the reinforcements are mountain troops that have taken a quick paratroop course.

17 May The British cruiser HMS *Effingham* runs aground and is lost south of Narvik. A battalion of troops to reinforce Bodø is taken back to Harstad when all its equipment is lost.

21 May Allies advance in the south to ring Narvik in. RAF No. 262 Squadron arrives at Bardufoss to fly air cover for the Allied force.

24 May Situation for the Allied armies in northern France is desperate. Allied Supreme War Council decides to end the Norway campaign and withdraw all forces. Narvik can be taken, but the port is to be destroyed to prevent its use for shipping Swedish iron ore.

26 May The British anti-aircraft cruiser HMS *Curlew* is sunk by air attack near Harstad.

27–28 May Norwegian and Allied forces attack Narvik, entering the town after a short fight. Generalleutnant Dietl's force retreats east, almost to Swedish border. During the final attack Luftwaffe bombers attacking from Trondheim carry out strikes on the Allied ships. The cruiser HMS *Cairo* is hit and severely damaged.

27 May Luftwaffe bombs the British base at Bodø, inflicting heavy damage.

31 May The British force at Bodø is evacuated.

June 1940

1 June France and Britain inform Norway of their plans to evacuate the country.

4 June Allied evacuations begin at Harstad. Bad weather from 2 to 6 June prevents German bombers from observing or bombing the departing troop convoys.

7 June The Norwegian government goes into exile aboard the British cruiser HMS *Devonshire*.

8 June German naval forces launch Operation *Juno* to relieve pressure on the Narvik garrison and, after discovering the evacuation, shift the mission to hunt and sink the aircraft carrier HMS *Glorious* and two escorting destroyers. *Scharnhorst*, damaged by a torpedo, returns to Trondheim.

9 June Norwegian military forces are ordered to cease resistance.

10 June The surrender is complete, and resistance is ended.

ATTACKER'S CAPABILITIES

The Luftwaffe in the lightning conquest

The German naval air arm

The main Luftwaffe force employed in the Norway campaign was X Fliegerkorps, which was created from the Luftwaffe's specialist naval air units and reinforced with fighter, Stuka and transport units for the operation. Much like Britain's Fleet Air Arm and RAF Coastal Command, Germany's naval air arm was the 'Cinderella service' of the Luftwaffe. Germany had built a large and very capable naval air service in World War I, fielding some innovative reconnaissance aircraft and some advanced seaplane fighters. Germany also developed seaplane bombers and, by the end of the war, was building aircraft carriers. From 1920 to 1935, the German Navy was forbidden to have an air arm by the Versailles Treaty, but the naval staff secretly maintained a small cadre of naval aviators for eventual rearmament. When the Luftwaffe was formally established in 1935, the shadow air arms of the army and navy were incorporated into the Luftwaffe, which determined how units would be organized and allocated. Luftwaffe commander-in-chief Hermann Göring insisted that he be in full control of 'his' Luftwaffe and was reluctant to approve more than a minimal naval air arm under the Kriegsmarine's operational control. Kriegsmarine commander-in-chief Admiral Raeder was very much a traditional battleship admiral and did not press Göring to build a strong naval air arm. By the summer of 1939, the Luftwaffe's naval air arm had a mere 200 operational aircraft divided into five naval air groups and five separate squadrons based along Germany's northern coast.

Many of the naval air squadrons were equipped with the obsolete He 59 seaplanes. The Dornier Do 18 flying boats were allocated to some squadrons, and the short-range Arado Ar 196 seaplane, used for reconnaissance and spotting, was just entering service. The best aircraft of the naval air arm was the Heinkel He 115 twin-engine seaplane that could carry a bombload of 1,250kg and had a range of 2,100km. Its range and ability to carry bombs, mines or torpedoes made it an especially important part of the Norway campaign where it served primarily in the reconnaissance role.

Bf 110Ds in formation. With a top speed of 336mph and an armament of two 20mm cannon and four 7.92mm machine guns in the nose, with a rear-firing 7.92mm machine gun operated by the radioman, the twin engine Me 110 was designed as the Luftwaffe's bomber escort. The Bf 110D had an extra fuel tank in the aircraft's belly, giving it a pregnant look, but also a range of 1,500km. The extra range of this model was essential for operations in Norway. Due to its lack of manoeuvrability, the Bf 110 did not perform well against single-engine fighters. However, it served very effectively as a night fighter, fighter bomber and reconnaissance aircraft. (Keystone via Getty Images)

A Heinkel He 115 being lifted by a crane. The twin-engine He 115 had a three-man crew and a range of 2,100km. With a bombload of 1,250kg, it could be used as a patrol bomber. The He 115 was the Luftwaffe's primary long-range naval reconnaissance aircraft and performed good service in Norway. (HMSO/Public domain)

General Hans Ferdinand Geisler (right) with Italian General Francesco Pricolo (left). Photo taken in 1941 after X Fliegerkorps was transferred to Italy. Geisler, a former navy officer and pilot with long experience in naval aviation, was a very capable commander of X Fliegerkorps in Norway in 1940. (Heinrich Hoffmann/Mondadori via Getty Images)

At the start of the war, the German naval air arm lacked an effective long-range anti-shipping capability. Luftwaffe senior commanders and general staff had lobbied Göring for years to create a modern naval air strike force and had been ignored. Hitler had believed that Britain would accept Germany's dominant position on the continent, so there would be no need to focus on war plans against Britain. Only in early 1938 was Britain added to the list of possible enemies and intelligence collection and war planning developed. Commander of Luftflotte 2, General Helmuth Felmy, carried out a series of wargames and exercises in 1938 and 1939 and concluded that if war with Britain came, the best use of air power would be a naval air campaign to mine British waters and attack shipping. Felmy and the Luftwaffe General Staff lobbied Göring to establish a long-range naval strike force equipped with the Dornier Do 217 bomber being developed, a better version of the fast Do 17 bomber then in service. Felmy's persistence paid off, and at the start of the war Luftflotte 2 formed X Fliegerkorps as a specialist anti-shipping force under command of the experienced naval airman Lt General Hans Geisler. The air division was assigned KG 26, equipped with He 111s, and KG 30, equipped with the Ju 88 medium bombers just entering service. After the Polish campaign, KG 4, equipped with He 111s but being re-equipped with Ju 88s, was assigned to X Fliegerkorps.

Oberstleutnant Martin Harlinghausen, the Luftwaffe's top anti-shipping expert, had been named by General Felmy as operations officer for Luftflotte 2 in April 1939. In October he was transferred to be X Fliegerkorps chief of staff. It was a sound move to ensure the buildup and training of X Fliegerkorps. Harlinghausen had joined the navy in 1923 and was commissioned a lieutenant in 1927. Having served as a surface officer, he took pilot training in 1931 and after transferring to the Luftwaffe in 1933 worked with General Geisler as a naval aviation specialist. After a tour teaching at the Luftwaffe Akademie, in January 1938 he took command of the Condor Legion's AS/88 Squadron, where he led the squadron's twin-engine He 59 seaplane bombers in strikes against both land and naval targets. Squadron AS/88 performed effectively in both roles, with Harlinghausen often leading missions. By the end of the Spanish war, AS/88 had been credited with sinking 52 Spanish Republican ships. As chief of staff of X Fliegerkorps, Harlinghausen again personally led anti-shipping strikes against British merchant shipping along Britain's east coast. From September 1939 to March 1940, 30 British merchant vessels were sunk, mostly small coasting vessels but also some large freighters. X Fliegerkorps also had a great deal to learn about coordination with the navy. In February 1940, the Kriegsmarine sent a flotilla of six destroyers for a sweep into the North Sea. Not having been notified of the naval operations in their area, patrols of X Fliegerkorps misidentified the destroyers as British and initiated an attack. The German destroyer *Z1 Leberecht Maas* was sunk, and another destroyer was either struck by German bombs or hit a mine – no one could be sure. It was a very bloody 'friendly fire' incident, but the Kriegsmarine and Luftwaffe quickly learned to coordinate their operations.

By the time of *Weserübung*, some of X Fliegerkorps' bomber groups had been well trained in anti-shipping operations by Harlinghausen, with KG 26 and KG 30 having the most experience. KG 4, equipped with He 111s, only

joined the command a few weeks before *Weserübung*. Even after the start of the war, Göring was reluctant to allow resources to be diverted to the aerial mining campaign or to the anti-shipping role. It was only due to General Felmy's insistence, and the leadership of General Geisler and Oberstleutnant Harlinghausen, that Germany had any well-equipped naval air units at all.

For the Norway operation X Fliegerkorps received some essential reinforcements. A group of single-engine Bf 109 fighters (II./JG 77 – approximately 40 aircraft) was added to protect the key Norwegian airfields from expected British bomber attacks. A group of Bf 110D twin-engine fighters (I./ZG 76) was added to provide fighter escort for the bombers and transports of X Fliegerkorps. The D model of the Bf 110 had an additional fuel tank that extended its already considerable range. A further major addition to X Fliegerkorps was a group of Ju 87R dive bombers (I./StG 1). The Stukas were the Luftwaffe's most effective anti-shipping bombers but had a very limited range. The Ju 87R model used by I./StG 1 was modified to carry extra fuel and to fly long-range missions.

Luftwaffe transport forces

Both the Luftwaffe's paratroop and transport forces proved to be decisive factors in the 1940 Norway campaign. Yet these two forces had been created almost by chance. In 1933, as Germany began rapid rearmament, the newly founded Air Ministry – headquarters for a Luftwaffe not yet officially established – proposed a plan for Germany to create a bomber force by acquiring large numbers of civilian airliners and cargo craft already in production and converting them into improvised bombers. The best aircraft available at the time was the Junkers Ju 52 transport, which had appeared in 1932 and was already in serial production. The Ju 52 could carry 17 passengers or 3 tons of cargo and had already earned a high reputation as a rugged, easy-to-fly, very efficient transport plane. It was simple to convert the Ju 52s into improvised bombers, so production was immediately expanded. The Ju 52 would become the mainstay of the Luftwaffe bomber force from 1934 to 1937, when brand-new, purpose-built bombers became available.

The improvised Ju 52 bombers were only a stopgap solution to organize and train bomber wings until they could be equipped with effective modern bombers. In 1936, the excellent Heinkel He 111 medium bomber started production and, along with the Dornier Do 17, began to re-equip the Luftwaffe's bomber formations. Another excellent medium bomber, the Junkers Ju-88, was in development. By 1937 the Luftwaffe no longer needed the Ju 52s as bombers so they were converted back to their original purpose as passenger and cargo aircraft. During history's first major military airlift in the Spanish Civil War, the Luftwaffe had seen the effectiveness of the Ju 52 as a transport plane. The German-led transport effort featuring the Ju 52s enabled the Spanish Nationalists to move thousands of troops and tons of weapons and munitions onto the Spanish mainland in 1936. Thanks to this effort the Nationalists took the offensive, eventually defeating the Spanish Republicans. As Luftwaffe bomber units converted to He 111s and Do 17s in 1936–37, the Luftwaffe found itself with hundreds of effective transport aircraft, which it incorporated into the Luftwaffe organization.

During the Polish campaign, the availability of hundreds of Ju 52 transports was a godsend to the Luftwaffe air fleets. Unlike the Western Allies, the German Army and Luftwaffe had a doctrine of mobile warfare, so the Luftwaffe had created more than 100 motorized supply companies and airfield units capable of moving into captured territory to set up airfields and begin immediate operations. While Luftwaffe medium bombers had the range to fly from established German airfields, half the Luftwaffe's aircraft were short-range

Formation of Heinkel He 111s over Norway. The He 111 was first used in Spain in 1937 and proved to be a highly effective medium bomber. With a top speed of 270mph, a 2,000kg bombload and range of 2,300km it was the main bomber of the Luftwaffe from 1939 to 1941. Although it could carry eight machine guns for defence, it was still highly vulnerable to fighter aircraft and required escort fighters to survive. The elite KGr 100 pathfinder unit was equipped with He 111s. (ullstein bild via Getty Images)

The Heinkel He 59, a twin-engine bomber seaplane, was useful for delivering troops and supplies in the narrow fjords of Norway. The He 59 had been successful as a bomber in the Spanish War, but by 1940 it was clearly obsolete in that role. However, it could carry up to 1,600kg of cargo or several soldiers. (Author's collection)

aircraft: fighters, ground attack planes and dive bombers. For the Luftwaffe to support the army, short-range aircraft needed the ability to deploy to temporary advanced bases. The Luftwaffe's logistics structure, with airfield companies and supply columns, made this possible. But as the Wehrmacht advanced into Poland in 1939, supply columns often could not bring fuel and munitions forward quickly. As a result, all major air commands used the air transport groups to fly fuel and munitions to forward bases so short-range fighters and Stukas could support the army. Luftwaffe transports also flew fuel forward to supply panzer units that had outrun their supply lines. The availability of hundreds of transports had been one of the factors that had made blitzkrieg possible. When planning began for *Weserübung* in December 1940, it was decided that most of Germany's transport forces would be needed to fly in troops, equipment and supplies on the first days. German planners could safely assume that the Luftwaffe transport force would perform as it had done in Poland.

The Fallschirmjäger

The motivation for the creation of Germany's paratroop forces came from the ego of Reichsmarschall Hermann Göring. As commander-in-chief of the Luftwaffe, in 1935 Göring decreed that the Luftwaffe should form a special infantry regiment to serve as a guard for Göring himself and his Air Ministry. He expected to display his beautifully uniformed Luftwaffe guards at the grand reviews and military parades characteristic of the Third Reich. The Luftwaffe's career officers had no choice but to defer to Göring's ego and create the unit. At the same time, they were aware of the successful experiments conducted by the Soviet Army in the dropping of paratroops. They decided that rather than forming a show infantry regiment – something that added nothing to the Luftwaffe's capabilities – the Luftwaffe's infantry should be paratroopers. A small paratroop force was quickly formed and participated in the Wehrmacht manoeuvres of 1936–37. During manoeuvres, the paratroop concept was proved successful in allowing the Wehrmacht to seize strategic targets such as airfields and

Paratroops in Norway. The 1940 campaign saw the world's first use of paratroops, used to seize strategic airfields in Denmark and Norway. The Germans conducted seven paratroop drops in the Norwegian campaign; all but the attempted seizure of the Dombås rail junction were successful. The ability to seize strategic targets deep behind enemy lines revolutionized warfare. The seizure of Aalborg and Stavanger airfields on 9 April by airborne landings were decisive moments in the campaign that assured Germany of air superiority. (Author's collection)

rail junctions deep in the enemy's rear. Thus, the original plan for a single infantry regiment expanded to creating an entire paratroop division, which became the 7. Fallschirmjäger-Division in the Luftwaffe organization. Together with hundreds of Ju 52 transports converted back to their original form, Germany found itself with the largest, most capable paratroop force in the world. A second division, the 22. Luftlande-Division (22nd Air Landing Division), was also created. This force would allow thousands of soldiers to be carried by gliders deep into the enemy's rear to seize strategic targets. The airborne/air-landing concept was already well established in the Wehrmacht and these forces were assigned a major role to seize targets deep inside the Netherlands at the opening of the spring offensive. Denying the *Weserübung* planners' request for the whole paratroop/air-landing force, the Army High Command assigned one reinforced battalion, I. Battalion/1. Fallschirmjäger-Regiment, to support the Norway operation. Without the transport and paratroop forces being readily available and already practised in the mission, the concept of *Weserübung* would have been simply impossible.

German paratroops in training, 1940, after the German paratroopers had landed, carrying only their pistols and hand grenades. Their rifles, heavier weapons and ammunition were dropped by parachute in special containers, which had to be retrieved after the drop. Germany had a large and well-trained paratroop and glider-landed force (two divisions) in 1940, in contrast to the Allies who had no such forces. (Bettmann/Getty Images)

German commanders

The German operational commanders had the advantage of Norway being a secondary theatre, with the attention of the army and Luftwaffe focused on the upcoming spring offensive. Only for the Kriegsmarine was Norway a primary theatre. Once the decision was made to invade Norway and the forces allocated, the operational commanders were largely left alone to plan and direct the campaign. The German Army and Luftwaffe benefited from the recent Polish campaign, where many lessons had been learned about air/ground cooperation and planning. General von Falkenhorst had commanded a corps in that campaign. Another key German commander, Lieutenant Colonel Martin Harlinghausen, chief of staff of X Fliegerkorps, had served a year in Spain as a squadron commander with the Condor Legion. The war experience of the German Army and air staffs was recent. In contrast, the last operational-level combat experience for the British chiefs, Army General Ironside and RAF Air Marshal Newall, had been more than two decades before.

GERMAN ORDER OF BATTLE, 9 APRIL 1940

Luftflotte 5 (after 12 April)
X Fliegerkorps
Bomber units
KG 4: Three groups equipped with 100
He 111P bombers
  Staff Flight
  I./KG 4
  II./KG 4
  III./KG 4
KG 26: Three groups equipped with 100
He 111P bombers

  Staff Flight
  I./KG 26
  II./KG 26
  III./KG 26
KG 30: Three groups equipped with 100
Ju 88 bombers:
  Staff Flight
  I./KG 30
  II./KG 30
  III./KG 30

OPPOSITE LUFTWAFFE AIR OPERATIONS 9 APRIL

Transport units
Air Transport Group Land: Commander Lt Col
von Gablenz
Six groups of Ju 52 transports: 322 aircraft
  KGr zbV 101
  KGr zbV 102
  KGr zbV 103
  KGr zbV 104
  KGr zbV 106
  KGr zbV 107
  KGr zbV 105 (six Ju 90, one G 38, four Fw 200)
KG zbV 1: Commander Lt Col Morzik
Four groups of Ju 52 transports: approximately
215 aircraft

Fighters, dive bombers and pathfinders
KGr 100   (Specially equipped pathfinder unit), one
             group He 111H bombers
I./StG 1   approximately 40 Ju 87R dive bombers
II./JG 77   approximately 40 Bf 109E fighters
I./ZG 76   40 Bf 110 heavy fighters

**Long-range reconnaissance force (approximately
24 aircraft)**
I./FAGr 120   Dornier 17P and He 111H bombers
I./FAGr 122   Dornier 17P and He 111H bombers

Army cooperation units
2(H)/20 2 Staffel Heeresfliegergruppe/20 (2nd
Squadron Army Reconnaissance Group 20): ten Hs 126
reconnaissance planes

Naval aviation units
Kü Fl Gr 506   three squadrons of He 115 seaplanes –
50 aircraft (used as reconnaissance and transports)
KGr zbV 108   He 59 twin-engine seaplanes and Ju 52s
modified as seaplanes – approximately 30 aircraft
Luftflotte 5 (support units)
Luftwaffe Signal Regiment 40
  Field Luftgau* 200
  Field Luftgau 300
Airborne units
  I. Battalion, 1. Fallschirmjäger-Regiment
(7. Fallschirmjäger-Division)

Kriegsmarine
Battleships: *Gneisenau, Scharnhorst*
Narvik, Marine Gruppe 1: ten destroyers: Z2, Z9, Z11,
Z12, Z13, Z17, Z18, Z19, Z21, Z22
Trondheim, Marine Gruppe 2: heavy cruiser *Admiral
Hipper;* 2. Destroyer Flotilla: Z5, Z6, Z8, Z16
Bergen, Marine Gruppe 3: cruisers *Köln, Königsberg;*
gunnery training ship *Bremse;* two torpedo boats;
1. S-Boat Flotilla – S-Boat Tender *Carl Peters,* S19, S21,
S22, S23, S24, Schiff 9, Schiff 18
Kristiansand and Arendal, Marine Gruppe 4: cruiser
Karlsruhe, three torpedo boats;
2. S-Boat-Flotilla – S-Boat-Tender Tsingtau, S7, S8, S17,
S30, S31, S32, S33
Oslo, Marine Gruppe 5 – heavy cruiser *Blücher,* heavy
cruiser *Lützow,* light cruiser *Emden,* three torpedo boats,
R7–R19, R22
Egersund, Marine Gruppe Six: 2. Minesweeping
Flotilla: M-1, M-2, M-9, M-13
German U-boat force: 30 U-boats available for North
Sea operations

Army forces
**German ground forces: General der Infanterie
Nikolaus von Falkenhorst, Commander Gruppe XXI
German Army committed to Norway (five infantry
divisions, two mountain divisions)**
Gruppe XXI (Group XXI built from XXI Corps
Headquarters)
1st Wave: 69. Infanterie-Division, 163. Infanterie-
Division, 3. Gebirgs-Division
2nd Wave: 181. Infanterie-Division, 196. Infanterie-
Division, 214. Infanterie-Division
Reserve
Panzer-Abteilung 40: 25 tanks
Corps troops
Schwere Artillerie Battalion 730 (730th Heavy Artillery
Battalion)
Signals, engineer and flak troops
Committed as reinforcements 21 April: 2. Gebirgs-
Division (2nd Mountain Division)
* A Luftgau controlled Luftwaffe administrative units,
airfield support and engineering units and other
attached forces such as Flak units.

Norwegian Sea

● Trondheim

Luftwaffe airfields and units, 9 April 1940

BOMBER AND DIVE-BOMBER UNITS

KG 4 (He 111P)

	Base	Target
Gruppe I	Perleberg	Overfly Denmark, attack Oscarsborg Oslo
Gruppe II	Fassberg	Oslo
Gruppe III	Lüneburg	7. Staffel, Oscarsborg
		8. Staffel, Stavanger
		9. Staffel, Bergen

KG 26 (He 111H)

Gruppe I	Wilhelmshaven-Varel	Kristiansand (2. & 3. Staffeln)
Gruppe II	Friedeburg-Marx	North Sea, RN Home Fleet
Gruppe III	Westerland-Sylt	Oslo

KG 30 (Ju 88A)

Gruppe I and II	Westerland-Sylt	North Sea, RN Home Fleet
Gruppe III	Friedeburg- Marx	North Sea, RN Home Fleet

KGr 100

	Nordholz, Schleswig	North Sea, RN Home Fleet

StG 1 (Ju 87)

	Kiel	Oscarsborg, Oslo Fjord. On afternoon of 9 April, partly redeployed to Stavanger to attack British shipping in North Sea

FIGHTER UNITS

ZG 76 (Bf 110)

	Base	Target
Gruppe I	Westerland (Sylt Island)	1. Staffel escort to Fornebu Oslo; 3. Staffel:Denmark/Stavanger

MARITIME RECONNAISSANCE UNITS

Kü Fl Gr 506 (He 115s)

	Base	Target
1. Staffel	Norderny (Friesland Islands)	North Sea reconnaissance
2. Staffel	Sylt Island	North Sea reconnaissance
3. Staffel	Sylt Island	North Sea reconnaissance

TRANSPORTS

	Base	Target
KGr zbV 101 (Ju 52)	Neumünster Oldenburg	Oslo, air-land infantry/Luftwaffe personnel
KGr zbV 102 (Ju 52)	Neumünster Oldenburg	Oslo, air-land infantry/Luftwaffe personnel
KGr zbV 103 (Ju 52)	Schleswig	Oslo, air-land infantry
KGr zbV 104 (Ju 52)	Stade	Stavanger, air-land troops
KGr zbV 105 (Fw 200 Condor, Ju 90, G 38)	Kiel	Trondheim, transport Luftwaffe personnel/equipment
KGr zbV 106 (Ju 52)	Ütersen	Stavanger, air-land troops
KGr zbV 107 (Ju 52)	Fuhlsbüttel	Oslo, air-land infantry/Luftwaffe personnel
KG zbV 108 (He 59, Ju 52 seaplane)	Hornum Sylt:	Bergen and Trondheim, air-land personnel/equipment

KG zbV 1 (Ju 52)

Gruppe I	Ütersen	Denmark: Storstrøm Bridge and Aalborg, paratroop drop, air-land infantry
Gruppe II	Ütersen	Oslo-Fornebu, paratroop drop
Gruppe III	Hagenow	Stavanger, paratroop drop & Aalborg Falster, Denmark, paratroop drop
Gruppe IV	Hagenow	Aalborg, air-land troops

German Airfields April 1940

1. Norderny
2. Wilhelmshaven
3. Oldenburg
4. Fassberg (Bremen)
5. Nordholz
6. Stade
7. Uetersen
8. Fuhlsbüttel (Hamburg)
9. Westerland/Sylt
10. Schleswig
11. Kiel
12. Lüneburg
13. Hagenow
14. Perleberg

● Bergen

● Oslo

● Stavanger

● Kristiansand

● Aalborg

DEFENDER'S CAPABILITIES
The Norwegians and their allies

The Norwegian armed forces

For most of the interwar period, Norway – a neutral nation during World War I – had been governed mostly by leftist governments that provided little funding for the armed forces and had little interest in Norwegian defence. Like the other Nordic nations, Norway had conscription, but with only 90 days of training, it had the shortest period for its conscript forces of all the Nordic nations. The Norwegian Army had only a small regular cadre force and was based around reserve forces, who received occasional training. When mobilized, reservists reported to local reserve centres. The Norwegian Army was organized into six infantry divisions which were primarily administrative units. The actual operational unit of the Norwegian Army was the infantry regiment. Each infantry division contained two to three infantry regiments, and an artillery regiment or battalion, along with a cavalry battalion. A few additional support troops, such as engineers, were included as well. None of the Norwegian Army's officers had war experience. The last experience the army had was partial mobilization for defence of Norwegian neutrality during World War I.

When World War II began, some Norwegian units were mobilized, mainly to guard the border in the far north with the Soviet Union in fear of a spillover from the war between Finland and Russia. The Norwegian government took few steps to improve the defence of Norway when the war broke out in 1939, believing that neutrality would again protect them from external intervention. The Norwegian Navy – surprisingly, for a maritime nation – was mostly a collection of ancient warships, the largest ships dating back to the 1890s and the first period of Norway's independence from Sweden. The only modern ships possessed by Norway were four small destroyers built in the 1930s. Otherwise, Norway's naval capabilities were minimal.

Norway had a separate naval air arm with three small squadrons that included some modern flying boats, such as the Heinkel 115 seaplane. The Norwegian Air Force (a branch of the army), like the military in general, had been under-funded and neglected. The best aircraft in the Norwegian Air Force was the Gloster Gladiator fighter, one squadron of which had been only recently acquired. The mainstay of the Norwegian Air Force were three squadrons of Fokker CV two-seater biplanes, which served as light bombers and reconnaissance planes. The Fokker CVs came into service in the mid-1920s and were hopelessly obsolete. At the beginning of the war, the air force contracted some American Curtiss P-36 fighters, which would have been an exponential improvement in Norwegian air defences. However, the six P-36s that had arrived were still crated and yet to be assembled.

Norwegian naval defences consisted of several concrete forts with heavy guns and torpedoes, which had been built in the first days of Norwegian independence at the beginning

Anti-aircraft gun mounted on a cargo ship of the Norwegian merchant marine, which played an important role supporting Allied operations in Norway, and then later during the Battle of the Atlantic. In 1940 more than a dozen Norwegian merchant vessels supporting the Allies were lost, many lost to Luftwaffe bombs. (Dahlberg/Three Lions/Getty Images)

of the 20th century. By 1940 the forts were mostly obsolete. Most heavy guns were not protected from air attack, nor did coastal forts have defences to protect them from infantry coming over land. Anti-aircraft protection for the nation was minimal, with Oslo having fewer than 20, older 75mm anti-aircraft guns available. Norwegian coastal forts lacked anti-aircraft protection beyond heavy machine guns. The Norwegian Army itself, being mainly a reserve force, could count on some excellent human materiel, since most Norwegians could ski competently, and many could hunt. Norwegians already had skills to be soldiers, and with training were potentially first-rate troops. However, the army's equipment was both obsolete and minimal. While the infantry was adequately armed with older-model bolt-action rifles and light and heavy machine guns, the artillery was obsolete. The army also lacked anti-aircraft guns, vehicles and heavy equipment. Norway had not a single tank or – even more importantly – a single anti-tank gun in the entire country.

The Danish forces

Denmark had a small army based on conscription, with considerably better equipment and training than the Norwegian Army. The Army Air Force of Denmark had four squadrons, and the navy had two air squadrons. It was a small navy of coastal defence ships and torpedo boats. As Denmark surrendered so quickly, its forces can scarcely be noted as a factor in the campaign.

The Allies

The British would contribute the majority of the foreign air forces that attempted to defend Norway. The Fleet Air Arm was specifically tasked to support the Royal Navy, which was responsible for gaining control of the sea and ensuring the transport of Allied

NORWEGIAN ARMY ORDER OF BATTLE

(six divisions and assorted cavalry and artillery and engineer units)
The Royal Guards Battalion
1st Division – HQ Halden: three infantry regiments
2nd Division – HQ Oslo: three infantry regiments

3rd Division – HQ Kristiansand: two infantry regiments
4th Division – HQ Bergen: two infantry regiments
5th Division – HQ Trondheim: three infantry regiments
6th Division – HQ Harstad: three infantry regiments

OPPOSITE RAF BOMBER COMMAND IN THE NORWAY CAMPAIGN

British troops pick through the ruins of Namsos after the major German air raid of 20 April 1940. The damage caused to the Allied logistics by air attacks convinced the Allied commanders that the British/French intervention in central Norway could not be maintained. (Captain Keating/Imperial War Museums via Getty Images)

troops and supplies to Norway. RAF Coastal Command, based on the east coast of England and Scotland, was tasked to conduct patrol and anti-shipping missions in the North Sea. RAF Bomber Command, based in southeastern England, had hardly been used up to this point in the war. It possessed the main force of British aircraft with the range to bomb targets in Norway, Denmark and northern Germany. RAF Fighter Command was marginal to the Norway operation because of the short range of its aircraft. However, two Fighter Command squadrons were used in Norway.

RAF Bomber Command

The pre-war doctrine of Bomber Command was to use bombers as a powerful long-range weapon to smash key German industries and forces in the homeland. Although RAF Bomber Command had over 1,000 aircraft available, before the Norway campaign they had contributed very little to Britain's military efforts. Under the orders of Prime Minister Neville Chamberlain, Bomber Command operated under strict rules of engagement that prohibited attacking any targets where civilians might be killed. Bomber Command's bombing operations were limited to attacking German naval bases in the North Sea, and the few small raids made on German naval forces inflicted minimal damage and cost the RAF heavy losses. The main activity of Bomber Command to April 1940 was to fly over western Germany and drop millions of propaganda leaflets with messages designed to demoralize the German population. Until the Battle of Norway and the German offensive in May 1940, the British government still entertained hopes that a peaceful solution could

Royal Air Force Bomber Command pilots return after bombing German warships at Bergen on 11 April 1940. Missions over the North Sea often encountered icing and zero visibility. Almost half the missions flown against German targets in April 1940 were changed or aborted en route due to weather conditions. (Keystone-France/Gamma-Keystone via Getty Images)

① Ports/number of raids

❶ Airfields/number of raids

N

0 — 100 miles

0 — 100km

NORWAY

Trondheim ② ❷ Trondheim Vaernes

① Bergen

Oslo (Fornebu) ❻ ❷ Oslo (Kjeller)
④
Oslo

② Stavanger
㉑ Stavanger Sola

Kristiansand
❶ ①

SHETLAND ISLANDS

ORKNEY ISLANDS

Skagerrak

❽ Aalborg

Kattegat

North Sea

SCOTLAND

❸ Rye

DENMARK

GREAT BRITAIN

Whitley

GERMANY

ENGLAND

Hampden

Blenheim

NETHERLANDS

Wellington

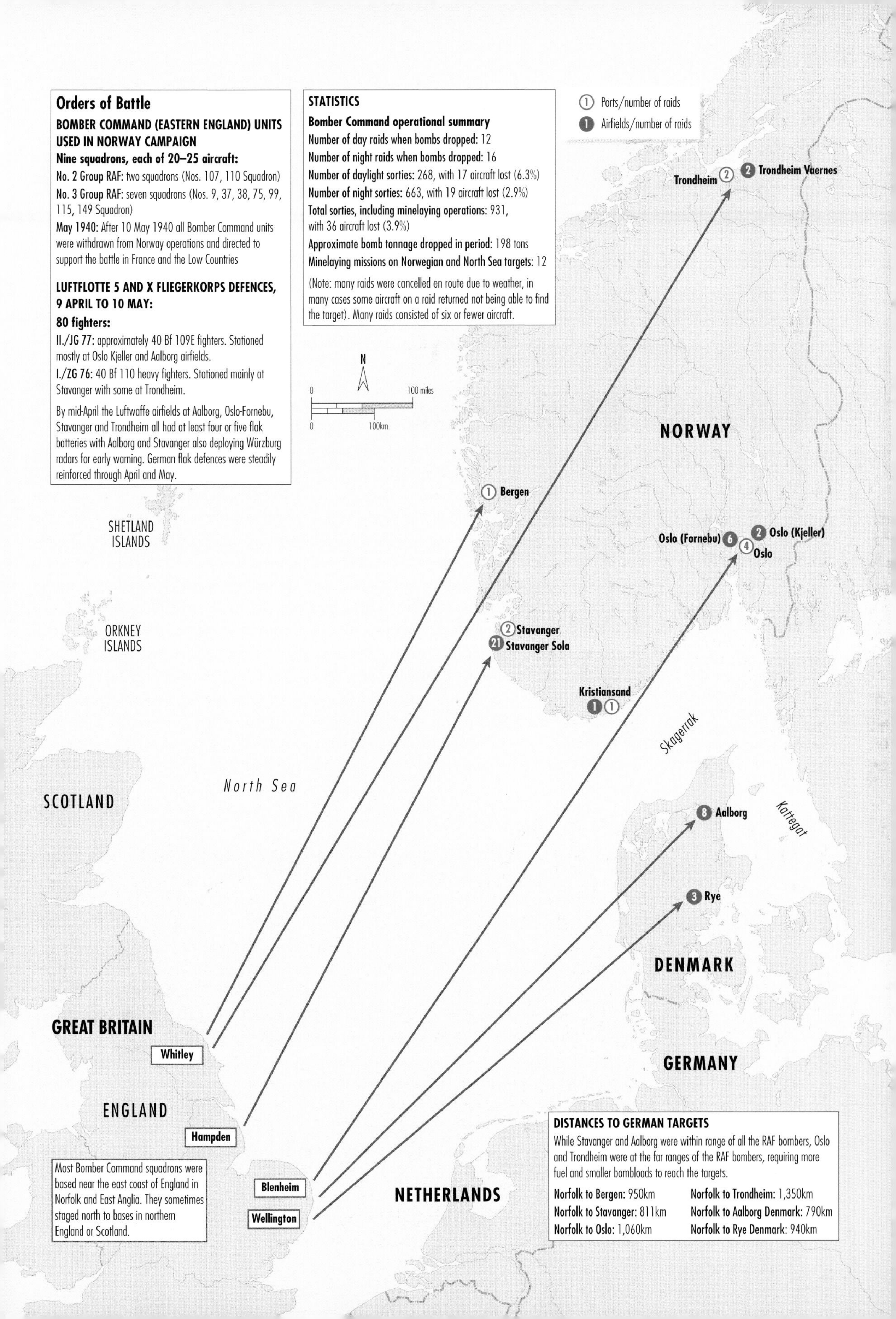

Most Bomber Command squadrons were based near the east coast of England in Norfolk and East Anglia. They sometimes staged north to bases in northern England or Scotland.

DISTANCES TO GERMAN TARGETS

While Stavanger and Aalborg were within range of all the RAF bombers, Oslo and Trondheim were at the far ranges of the RAF bombers, requiring more fuel and smaller bombloads to reach the targets.

Norfolk to Bergen: 950km

Norfolk to Stavanger: 811km

Norfolk to Oslo: 1,060km

Norfolk to Trondheim: 1,350km

Norfolk to Aalborg Denmark: 790km

Norfolk to Rye Denmark: 940km

Air Marshal Sir Charles Portal. Portal was one of the rising stars of the RAF, a highly intelligent but taciturn man described as completely unflappable. He took over Bomber Command on 2 April 1940 and adopted the policy of night bombing based on the Norway experience. Portal became Chief of the Air Staff in October 1940 and served through the war as chief of the RAF. (Keystone/Hulton Archive/Getty Images)

be found, so bombers were withheld from all but a few indirect military operations.

In April 1940 Bomber Command was one of the few British instruments of power that could swiftly attack. But after seven months of the 'phony war' the RAF had lost its aggressive edge. On 2 April 1940 Air Marshal Charles Portal was appointed as chief of Bomber Command in a routine change of appointment. He found a force that was largely obsolescent, equipped with Hampden, Whitley and Wellington medium bombers, and Blenheim light bombers. Of these types, only the Wellington would prove itself to be an effective aircraft for its era. The woeful performance of the others in Norway would lead to their withdrawal from front-line bomber service as soon as the RAF could afford it. Bomber Command also lacked the training to conduct long missions over the North Sea. Even worse, the RAF lacked basic maps and good intelligence on the German forces and bases. Despite the problems, it was in Norway that Bomber Command finally began serious war operations.

The British faced several serious operational problems that inhibited using the bombers in an effective manner. First, the weather conditions and the long distances involved in flying to Norway from British bases worked against them. To reach some targets the British would have to stage bomber units out of their main concentration of bomber bases in East Anglia and move them to a limited number of airbases in Scotland. From the Scottish bases, RAF bombers would then have to fly 1,000-mile (1,600km) missions in the bad spring weather over the North Sea. The range of the RAF's aircraft limited them to operating only against targets in southern Norway or Denmark. Despite having an offensive air doctrine built around the long-range bomber, the RAF lacked the training to carry out effective long-range operations in April 1940 and few RAF aircrew were adequately trained for long-distance navigation, or to fly at night. Furthermore, in 1940 there were few navigational aids available to the RAF.

Fleet Air Arm

During World War I, the British were the world leaders in naval aviation. Britain created a vast naval air arm and created the world's first aircraft carriers, including HMS *Hermes*, laid down during World War I and commissioned in 1924 as the world's first purpose-built aircraft carrier. However, in 1918, the Royal Naval Air Service was absorbed into the new Royal Air Force. It is notable that it was the Royal Naval Air Service that had pioneered many of the major air missions of the war, including strategic bombing and long-distance aviation.

Using the Royal Naval Air Service's World War I record as a model, the United States and Japanese navies built up their own naval air arms – not as part of a single air force, but as an integral part of their navies. After the war the US Navy and Japanese Navy eagerly took up the originally British concept of the aircraft carrier. Like the British, these two navies transformed some battle cruisers being built into aircraft carriers. Both America and Japan developed large and capable naval aviation forces, built around large aircraft carriers.

In Britain, while the navy had a Fleet Air Arm and provided the funding for aircraft carriers, the Royal Air Force and its budget controlled the acquisition of aircraft and the training of pilots for the Fleet Air Arm, which operated under Royal Navy command and control. For the Royal Air Force, naval aviation was a low priority for budget and personnel. By the outbreak of World War II Britain had seven aircraft carriers, mostly ships laid down as battlecruisers during World War I and commissioned in the 1920s. The only truly modern aircraft carrier of the Royal Navy in 1939 was HMS *Ark Royal*, which had been purpose-built as a carrier and commissioned in 1934.

After 20 years of rivalry, in late 1938 the Royal Navy won the administrative battle with the RAF and took over full control of the Fleet Air Arm. The obsolescence of the British carrier force, especially in comparison with the American and Japanese navies, was striking. A new class of aircraft carrier was being built thanks to rearmament funds in the late 1930s, but these would not be ready for the Norway campaign. In the Norway campaign, three British aircraft carriers would be available to support the Royal Navy: HMS *Furious*, *Glorious*, and *Ark Royal*.

The first big problem for the Fleet Air Arm was aircraft. While the Royal Air Force moved quickly to develop high-performance fighter and bomber monoplanes in the early 1930s, the RAF procured mediocre and obsolescent aircraft for the fleet's carriers. A mainstay of the Fleet Air Arm carrier force was the Fairey Swordfish biplane torpedo bomber, which entered service in 1936. It was an efficient torpedo bomber but very slow and already obsolete when built. In 1939 the navy had 13 front-line squadrons equipped with the Swordfish. The RAF procured for the navy a combination fighter plane and dive bomber, the Blackburn Skua, which entered service in November 1938. It was the Fleet Air Arm's first all-metal monoplane aircraft and expected to operate both as a fighter and dive bomber. The Skua was a thoroughly mediocre aircraft in both roles. As a fighter, it was extremely slow, with a maximum speed of 225mph – in contrast to the speed of the British and German fighter planes, which exceeded 300mph. As a fighter, it was lightly armed with four rifle-calibre Browning machine guns in the wing, and one Lewis gun in the rear cockpit. As a dive bomber, it could carry no more than one 500lb bomb. It could be more accurately described as a glide bomber, and with a shallow glide capability. The third aircraft of the Fleet Air Arm was the Gloster Gladiator, a biplane fighter first flown in 1934. Gladiators were modified for service aboard aircraft carriers and a small number were available for the navy. The Gladiator had a top speed of approximately 250mph, and its four machine guns could not match the armament of other German or British fighters.

British carriers were smaller and less capable than the Japanese and American carriers that served the fleet. The most modern British aircraft carrier, the *Ark Royal*, could carry 50–60 aircraft. In the *Ark Royal*'s case, it carried 26 Fairey Swordfish and 24 Blackburn Skuas. Corresponding Japanese and American fleet aircraft carriers carried 80–90 aircraft, and the Japanese and American naval fighter aircraft were more modern, faster and more capable than any of the aircraft possessed by the Royal Fleet Air Arm. In short, during the interwar period, neither the RAF nor the Royal Navy had stressed carrier operations for the fleet. While the Americans and Japanese worked out doctrine for operating two or more aircraft carriers together as a task force, and practised carrier task forces in large fleet manoeuvres, the practical training for the carrier forces in the Royal Navy languished.

Thus, during the Norway campaign, Britain was not well supported in terms of naval aviation and was not a first-class navy in terms of aviation. Britain's deficiencies in the size, numbers, aircraft and training of its carrier force would be decisive factors in the campaign. One can imagine a very different outcome if the Royal Navy, which had been so innovative at the beginning of naval aviation, had retained control of its naval air arm in the

Blackburn Skua Mk II dive bombers in formation. The Blackburn Skua served both as a fighter and a dive bomber for the Fleet Air Arm. It was a mediocre aircraft in both roles. Its poor performance in Norway led to it being taken out of service in summer 1940. (Charles E. Brown/Royal Air Force Museum/Getty Images)

OPPOSITE RAF COASTAL COMMAND NO. 18 GROUP, APRIL 1940

No. 18 Group Coastal Command was responsible for most of the North Sea and part of the North Atlantic and Norwegian Sea (boundaries shown). They faced off against the Luftwaffe reconnaissance/bomber forces of Luftflotte 2 and X Fliegerkorps.

interwar period and developed concepts of naval carrier operations the way the US Navy and Japan had done. Yet, even if all three British carriers in the Norway campaign had been used as a single task force, they would still have had fewer aircraft and far less capability than any two of the American or Japanese fleet carriers.

RAF Coastal Command became one of the major branches of the RAF during the reorganization of the mid-1930s. It had the responsibility to conduct maritime patrol and anti-shipping operations and was equipped with twin-engine land-based patrol bombers and flying boats capable of long-range operations. Squadrons were organized into a group, each of which was responsible for a sector of the sea around the British Isles. No. 18 Group Coastal Command was responsible for most of the North Sea region and in April 1940 consisted of ten squadrons. Coastal Command had the primary responsibility to monitor the sea along the Norwegian coast.

If the Fleet Air Arm was a 'Cinderella service' of the RAF, then Coastal Command was even more so. In 1940 the main aircraft for the patrol squadrons was the Avro Anson, a reliable but obsolete aircraft that lacked the range and bombload to be effective. The Anson was slated to be withdrawn from active operations as soon as better aircraft were procured, but it was still manufactured in large numbers because it made an excellent basic trainer for multi-engine aircraft crews. No. 18 Group had four squadrons of new Lockheed Hudsons, an American twin-engine airliner converted into a patrol bomber. The Hudson was superior to the Anson but was still a stopgap measure until better, purpose-built aircraft could be fielded. Early in the war Coastal Command still had some obsolete flying boats assigned to long-range patrol. No. 209 Squadron of No. 18 Group was still equipped with the Saunders-Roe A.36 Lerwick flying boat, a badly designed and difficult-to-fly aircraft that never should have made it to front-line service. Of 21 Lerwicks built, 11 were lost to operational accidents.

On the positive side, Coastal Command had started to re-equip flying boat squadrons with the superb Short Sunderland four-engine flying boat that had been developed from the large civilian passenger flying boats of the 1930s. With a range of 2,860km and able to carry a large load (2,250kg of bombs or depth charges), it made an excellent reconnaissance and anti-submarine platform. Slow, but equipped with 16 .303-calibre machine guns (it carried five gunners), it could defend itself against enemy fighters. No. 18 Group received its first Sunderlands in April 1940 when No. 204 Squadron was re-equipped with them. Some Sunderlands were also available for North Sea operations from other Coastal Command groups, with a detachment of No. 210 Squadron flying with No. 18 Group in the Norway campaign. The Sunderlands, like the German flying boats, were also capable of transporting troops and materiel. Unfortunately, Coastal Command had too few Sunderlands for its requirements, and it was limited as an anti-submarine weapon because the British anti-submarine bombs were not very effective. Later in the war, when Britain had developed very lethal anti-submarine bombs and equipped the Sunderlands with radar, they became a potent anti-submarine aircraft.

Gloster Gladiator fighter. Developed in the early 1930s, the Gloster Gladiator was Britain's last fighter biplane. With a top speed of only 255mph and armed with four machine guns, the Gladiator was obsolete in 1940. However, the Gladiators in Norwegian service and with RAF No. 263 Squadron, performed well against German bombers. (Charles E. Brown/Royal Air Force Museum/Getty Images) Coastal Command

RAF NO. 18 GROUP | HQ ROSYTH (approximately 200 aircraft)

Unit	Station	Aircraft
No. 201 Squadron	RAF Sullom Voe	Short Sunderland
No. 209 Squadron	RAF Invergordon	Saunders-Roe Lerwick
No. 220 Squadron	RAF Thornaby	Lockheed Hudson
No. 224 Squadron	RAF Leuchars	Lockheed Hudson
No. 233 Squadron	RAF Leuchars	Lockheed Hudson
No. 240 Squadron	RAF Invergordon	Saunders-Roe London
No. 269 Squadron	RAF Montrose	Avro Anson/Lockheed Hudson
No. 608 Squadron	RAF Thornaby	Avro Anson
No. 612 Squadron	RAF Dyce	Avro Anson

LUFTWAFFE X FLIEGERKORPS

Over 100 long-range reconnaissance aircraft, and 60-plus shorter-range reconnaissance aircraft.

Bases for long-range maritime reconnaissance

HQ X Fliegerkorps: Hamburg

Sylt: Kü Fl Gr 505

Norderny: Kü Fl Gr 505

Beginning on the afternoon of 9 April many of the long-range Luftwaffe reconnaissance aircraft of Kü FL Gr 505 were deployed to Stavanger and Bergen.

Trondheim

NORWAY

Bergen

RAF Sullom Voe

SHETLAND ISLANDS

Stavanger

ORKNEY ISLANDS

Boundaries of No. 18 Group's responsibility

Scapa Flow — RNAS Hatston

RAF Invergordon

Skagerrak

RAF Dyce

SCOTLAND

RAF Montrose

RAF Leuchars

North Sea

DENMARK

Rosyth, No. 18 Group HQ

18 Group Coastal Command Group Boundary

16 Group Coastal Command

Sylt

RAF Thornaby

GREAT BRITAIN

Norderny

Hamburg
X Fliegerkorps HQ

IRELAND

WALES

ENGLAND

NETHERLANDS

GERMANY

N

0   150 miles

0   150km

DISTANCES

The main purpose of the RAF's Coastal Command and the Luftwaffe's reconnaissance/patrol aircraft was to monitor ship movements in the North Sea and to attack enemy shipping when possible. By occupying Norway's key ports and airfields on 9 April and establishing new bases for air reconnaissance and patrol, the Luftwaffe gained an advantage in shortening the distance to its main reconnaissance objectives — the Royal Navy's Home Fleet bases at Scapa Flow and Rosyth. A shorter distance meant more sorties could be mounted. Narvik and the waters around Harstad were now within range of German bomber and reconnaissance aircraft based in Trondheim.

Sylt to Scapa Flow: 837km

Norderny to Scapa Flow: 927km

Norderny to Rosyth: 650km

Norderny to Narvik: 1,940km

Scapa Flow to Narvik: 1,794km

Sullom Voe to Narvik: 1,593km

Bergen to Scapa Flow: 509km

Bergen to Rosyth: 705km

Stavanger to Scapa Flow: 511km

Stavanger to Rosyth: 643km

Scapa Flow to Trondheim: 888km

Trondheim to Narvik: 984km

LUFTWAFFE RECONNAISSANCE/ARMED PATROL UNITS

Kü Fl Gr 505: three squadrons of He 115s at stations Norderny and Sylt

KGr 100: He 111s equipped for long-range navigation. These were routinely used to carry out long-range patrol.

KGr zbV 105: several Fw 200 Condors assigned, also used as long-distance reconnaissance.

All bomber wings had a flight of long-range reconnaissance Do 17s assigned. These were committed to North Sea patrol. The Luftwaffe also had several squadrons of short-range Arado 196 seaplanes based near Norderny and Sylt for covering the areas close to the German/Danish coast.

The chiefs of the three British services at 10 Downing Street in 1939: Field Marshal Sir Edmund Ironside (left), Air Marshal Sir Cyril Newall (centre) and First Sea Lord Sir Dudley Pound (right). All three men were talented in their way, but as a leadership team were completely ineffective. Ironside, while an experienced field commander, had never served at the strategic level. Newall, a talented RAF administrator, showed little interest in supporting army and navy operations. Admiral Pound was in poor health and had little interest in army and air operations. Their failure to understand joint operations with other services ensured that the British intervention in Norway was poorly planned and poorly supported. (Popperfoto via Getty Images/ Getty Images)

British commanders

The campaign in Norway was directed by the three service chiefs who met almost every day during the campaign. The campaign in Norway was, above all, a joint campaign in which success demanded that army, navy and air forces worked effectively together, following a well-coordinated plan and strategy. The chief of the Royal Navy was Admiral of the Fleet Sir Alfred Dudley Pound, the British Army's chief was General William Edmund Ironside, and the chief of the RAF was Air Marshal Cyril Newall. While the service records of these three men were solid, their personal characters and professional flaws made it impossible for the top British military leaders to work together to command an effective operation. Unfortunately for Britain, at the time it was well known among the senior officer ranks of all three services that their service chiefs were not the best men for the job. Their performance in Norway would lead to major changes in the top British military leadership.

ALLIED ORDER OF BATTLE, 9 APRIL 1940

Royal Air Force, Bomber Command
No. 2 Group: two squadrons (Nos. 107, 110)
No. 3 Group: seven squadrons (Nos. 9, 37, 38, 75, 99, 115, 149)
(After 10 May 1940, all Bomber Command units were withdrawn from Norway operations and directed to support the battle in France and the Low Countries)
Coastal Command No. 18 Group
Eight squadrons, of which the only effective were No. 204 Sqn with long-range Sunderland flying boats and three squadrons of Hudson patrol bombers
Allied ground forces
Mauriceforce – Major General Carton de Wiart V.C., landing at Namsos 14 April
British 146th (Territorial) Infantry Brigade – Commander Brigadier Charles Phillips

1/4th Battalion, Royal Lincolnshire Regiment, 1/4th Battalion, King's Own Yorkshire Light Infantry, Hallamshire Battalion, York and Lancaster Regiment

French 5e Demi-Brigade de Chasseurs Alpins – Commander Général de Brigade Antoine Béthouart: 13e Bataillon de Chasseurs Alpins, 53e Bataillon de Chasseurs Alpins, 67e Bataillon de Chasseurs Alpins

Sickleforce – Commander Major General Bernard Charles Paget

15th Infantry Brigade – 1st Battalion, Green Howards, 1st Battalion, King's Own Yorkshire Light Infantry, 1st Battalion, York and Lancaster Regiment

148th Infantry (Territorial) Brigade – Commander General Harold Morgan: 1/5th Battalion, Leicestershire Regiment, 1/8th Battalion, Sherwood Foresters, 168th Light Anti-Aircraft Battery, Royal Artillery, 260th Heavy Anti-Aircraft Battery, Royal Artillery, 55th Field Company, Royal Engineers

Rupertforce (Later Northwest Force) – Commander Major General Pierse Mackesy, after 13 May Commander Lieutenant General Claude Auchinleck

24th (Guards) Brigade, 1st Battalion, Scots Guards, 1st Battalion, Irish Guards, 2nd Battalion, South Wales Borderers

French 27e Demi-Brigade de Chasseurs Alpins: 6e Bataillon de Chasseurs Alpins, 12e Bataillon de Chasseurs Alpins, 14e Bataillon de Chasseurs Alpins

French 13th Foreign Legion Demi-Brigade: 1er Bataillon, 2e Bataillon

Polish Podhale (Rifle) Bde, 1st Demi-Brigade: 1 Battalion, 2 Battalion; 2nd Demi-Brigade: 3 Battalion, 4 Battalion

British: Troop, 3rd The King's Own Hussars, 203 Battery, 51st (Westmoreland and Cumberland) Field Regiment, Royal Artillery, British Nos. 1, 2, 3, 4, 5 Independent Companies ('Scissorsforce')

French: 342e Independent Tank Company, 2e Independent Colonial Artillery Group

Additional forces arrived in May

6th Anti-Aircraft Brigade, 51st (London) Heavy Anti-Aircraft Regiment, 82nd (Essex) Heavy Anti-Aircraft Regiment, Royal Artillery (156, 193, 256 Batteries), 55th (Devon) Light Anti-Aircraft Regiment, Royal Artillery (163, 164, 165 Batteries), 56th (East Lancashire) Light Anti-Aircraft Regiment, Royal Artillery (3, 167 Batteries) 229 and 230 Field Companies, Royal Engineers

Royal Navy Home Fleet, ships available on 9 April. The Home Fleet was one of several Royal Navy commands in the British Isles and could draw on support and reinforcements from other commands.

Four battleships: HMS *Resolution*, HMS *Rodney*, HMS *Valiant* and HMS *Warspite*

Two battlecruisers: HMS *Renown* and HMS *Repulse*

Three aircraft carriers: HMS *Furious* (HMS *Ark Royal* and HMS *Glorious* – detached to Mediterranean, returned 23 April)

Five heavy cruisers: HMS *Berwick*, HMS *Devonshire*, HMS *Effingham*, HMS *Suffolk* and HMS *York*

Five light cruisers: HMS *Birmingham*, HMS *Glasgow*, HMS *Manchester*, HMS *Sheffield* and HMS *Southampton*

Six anti-aircraft cruisers: HMS *Cairo*, HMS Calcutta, HMS *Carlisle*, HMS *Coventry*, HMS *Curacoa* and HMS *Curlew*

Seven Tribal-destroyers: HMS *Afridi* (sunk 3 May), HMS *Bedouin*, HMS *Cossack*, HMS *Eskimo*, HMS *Gurkha* (sunk 9 April), HMS *Punjabi* and HMS *Zulu*

14 destroyers: HMS *Acasta* (sunk 8 June), HMS *Ardent* (sunk 8 June), HMS *Forester*, HMS *Foxhound*, HMS *Glowworm* (sunk 8 April), HMS *Hardy* (sunk 10 April), HMS *Havock*, HMS *Hero*, HMS *Hostile*, HMS *Hotspur*, HMS *Hunter* (sunk 10 April), HMS *Icarus*, HMS *Kimberley*, HMS *Wolverine*

Four sloops: HMS *Auckland* (damaged 20 April), HMS *Bittern* (sunk 30 April), HMS *Black Swan*, HMS *Flamingo*, HMS *Fleetwood*, HMS *Stork*

17 submarines

Numerous minesweepers, armed trawlers of 300–700 GRT, armed merchant ships and supply vessels

French Navy

Two cruisers: *Émile Bertin* and *Montcalm*

Four auxiliary cruisers: *El Djezaïr*, *El Mansour*, *El Kantara*, *Ville d'Oran*

Nine destroyers: *Bison*, *Tartu*, *Maillé Brézé*, *Chevalier Paul*, *Boulonnais*, *Milan*, *Épervier*, *Brestois*, *Foudroyant*

17 transport ships

One submarine

Polish Navy – operating under British command

Three destroyers – *Błyskawica*, *Burza*, *Grom*

One submarine – *Orzeł*

Three troopships – MS *Chrobry*, MS *Sobieski*, MS *Batory*

CAMPAIGN OBJECTIVES

Here British soldiers watch an oil depot burning after German bomb strikes. All the ports used to support the British forces in Norway (Namsos, Harstad, Åndalsnes, Bodø, Molde) were heavily bombed. Destroying their supply bases made it impossible to maintain Allied forces in Norway. (R. Gates/Archive Photos/Getty Images)

German initial planning

A concept for the invasion of Norway was developed and showed promise. On 27 January 1940 Hitler ordered OKW to set up an operational planning staff for an invasion of Norway, which would be called *Weserübung* (Weser Exercise) and under the control of OKW. OKW ordered each service to provide an experienced staff officer, and Captain Theodor Kranke, a cruiser commander and experienced naval staff officer, became unofficial leader of the special staff, which was called 'Arbeitsgemeinschaft Kranke' (Planning Group Kranke). The senior Luftwaffe representative was Colonel Robert Knauss, a PhD in economics who had been a senior manager with Lufthansa and had returned to the Luftwaffe in 1935 and become a bomber group commander. The senior army planner was Major von Teppelskirche. The army and Luftwaffe were focused on planning for the great spring offensive, but the naval staff provided support for the planning group and close liaison with the other services.

By mid-February, the main elements of the plan were set out. A surprise attack would simultaneously seize all of Norway's major ports and airfields. Naval task forces would land troops at Oslo, Kristiansand, Bergen, Trondheim and Narvik. Paratroop units followed by air-landed infantry would seize the Oslo and Stavanger airports. Virtually all the German surface fleet would have to be used to land even a modest army force on Norwegian soil. Objectives had to be taken quickly, and in strength, as the British would mount a powerful counterstrike. It was determined early in the planning that Denmark would have to be invaded and occupied as well. The Luftwaffe required the two major airfields at Aalborg, located in the north of Denmark, to carry out air operations over Norway. German bomber and transport forces had the range to fly from northern Germany to southern Norway, but Stukas, fighters and short-range reconnaissance aircraft did not have the range to deploy to Norway and cover the army and navy. Holding Aalborg gave Luftwaffe bombers a greater range over the North Sea and central Norway and gave Stukas and fighters a refuelling point to fly on to Norwegian airfields. So, Gruppe Kranke drew up a plan to seize Denmark with a few regiments. Estimates for the forces to be used for the campaign were ready by mid-February. It was an impressive feat of operational planning.

Events pushed the Norway operation along. On 16 February, the Royal Navy attacked and boarded the German naval supply vessel *Altmark* that was sailing in Norwegian waters with a load of British prisoners taken by the pocket battleship *Graf Spee*. The Germans were put on alert that the British were ready to violate Norwegian neutrality to interdict German shipping. The Germans believed, quite correctly, that the British had plans to land troops in Norway to cut off Germany's ore supplies. It became a race to see which country got into Norway first. Another factor pushing the schedule of the campaign was the planned German offensive in the West. The Luftwaffe needed to carry out the Norway operation quickly so it could redirect forces to the campaign in the West. A campaign in Norway would require committing most of the Luftwaffe's transport forces, which would also be needed to support 'Fall Gelb', the forthcoming attack in France and the Low Countries. So, an attack on Norway had to be scheduled at least a couple of weeks before the offensive in the West.

On 19 February OKW was ordered to carry out the operation as soon as feasible. Army General der Infanterie Nikolaus von Falkenhorst, commander of XXI.Armee-Korps, was selected as the Norway invasion force commander. XXI.Armee-Korps, which had taken part in the Polish campaign, became headquarters for the Norway force staff and was renamed Gruppe XXI. Gruppe Kranke was incorporated into the staff as well. Luftwaffe support for the operation would be X Fliegerkorps, the Luftwaffe's specialist maritime operations force.

Unloading a Luftwaffe 88mm anti-aircraft gun at Kristiansand in early April 1940. The captured Norwegian Air Force airfield at Kristiansand became the home of a Me 109E fighter squadron tasked with the defence of southern Norway. Luftwaffe commanders Geisler, Milch and Stumpff put a high priority on rushing heavy and light flak guns to all the major German airfields. (Photo by Atlantic-Press/ullstein bild via Getty Images)

OPPOSITE
Colonel, later General, Robert Knauss. Knauss was the Luftwaffe's senior planner on the original planning group for *Weserübung*, serving for a time as chief of staff of X Fliegerkorps and as a bomber group commander. With a PhD in Economics, Knauss had long experience in German civil aviation before joining the Luftwaffe in the mid-1930s. He went on to become chief of the Luftwaffe's General Staff College. (Author's collection)

The British look to Norway

The British planning for intervention in Norway was driven by the Ministry of Economic Warfare. In October and November 1939 the ministry developed several studies that German arms production would be dealt a crippling blow if the iron-ore shipments from northern Sweden, much of which passed through the port of Narvik, could be cut off. The reports got the attention of the Cabinet and military staffs, and on 16 December Winston Churchill, First Lord of the Admiralty, presented a memo to the War Cabinet advocating mining Norwegian coastal waters to stop the flow of ore from Narvik. Two days later the British service chiefs recommended forces be prepared to intervene in Norway. In early January 1940, the service chiefs recommended a much larger force than first envisioned be readied for Norwegian intervention, and on 6 January 1940 the British Army ordered that some units be held ready for operations in Scandinavia. On 19 January operational planning began, codenamed 'Avonmouth'.

In contrast to that of the Germans, the British planning for intervention in Norway was neither well-staffed nor supported. At the strategic level in Britain, there was a Joint Planning Committee, responsible for developing plans for the anticipated Norway operation, but six months into the war there were only six officers assigned to the committee. An interservice planning staff had been formed before the war, but it had only three relatively junior officers assigned. By the end of January, the British draft plan, more of a concept than a plan, first assumed that Norwegians would accept Allied intervention and the British would not have to fight their way into Norway. The concept was to intervene in Norway, possibly occupy the iron mines in northern Sweden as well, with a force of 80,000 men and 10,000 vehicles under a corps headquarters. Only two air squadrons were assigned to support the first wave of the intervention force. Narvik was the focus of British effort, although it was anticipated that Stavanger would require an Allied force. The plan called for relying mostly upon the two brigades of the 49th Division of the Territorial Army (British Army reserve forces) and adding the regular army's 24th Brigade to the mix. The problem was that the Territorial Army that was to be the main intervention force was poorly trained and equipped and unready for combat.

On 5 February, the Allied Supreme War Council met in France, and the French were ready to provide army and navy units to serve under British command for an expeditionary force to Norway. While diplomatically the intervention was to be justified by helping Scandinavia protect itself against the Russian aggression against Finland, the real motivation of the Allies was to cut off the Swedish iron-ore shipments to Germany. Planning continued through March, but having identified units for the Norway expedition, the British command made no effort to provide additional training or equipment for the Territorial Army. The French offered their mountain troops for the expedition, but these units also were newly organized and not fully trained.

Final plans and preparations

By early March the German plan for Norway was finalized. The Army High Command allocated six infantry divisions for Norway – all units not needed for the upcoming offensive in the West. Five of the six divisions (69., 163., 181., 196. and 214. Infanterie-Divisions) were from the sixth and seventh mobilization waves and were newly formed with only a small cadre of regular officers and NCOs and led mostly by reserve officers. These divisions also had a smaller allotment of artillery and motor vehicles than earlier mobilization waves. However, all had completed unit and division training and were deemed combat-ready. The sixth division of Gruppe XXI was 3. Gebirgs-Division (3rd Mountain Division), a highly trained and specially equipped mountain unit, ideal for the Norwegian terrain. It was also a veteran division that had fought in the Polish campaign. Since the Army High Command would not release any panzer or motorized troops for the Norway invasion, the *Weserübung* planners quickly organized a small provisional tank battalion composed of obsolete tanks taken from the Panzer training centre and manned by soldiers from the training centre. Such a unit was not deemed adequate to fight against the Western Allies in the spring, but against a Norwegian army that had no tanks or anti-tank guns, it was 'good enough'.

Loading bombs onto a Ju 87. The establishment of a robust Luftwaffe logistics system in the first days of the invasion meant that the Luftwaffe could maintain a high sortie rate and had enough munitions to support intensive operations. (Author's collection)

The Luftwaffe's X Fliegerkorps would provide more than 500 combat aircraft for Norway, three bomber wings, three fighter groups, a Stuka group, as well as long-range reconnaissance squadrons and the naval air reconnaissance group. Just as importantly, more than 500 of the Luftwaffe's transport aircraft, more than half the available transports, were assigned to support the Norway invasion, at least in the early days. The Luftwaffe would also allocate one battalion of paratroops for the operation. Paratroops would seize the key airfields needed by the invasion force at the start of the operation, but after would be returned to their parent division to be part of the spring offensive.

By early March the German plan was essentially complete. While hoping the Norwegian government would cave and allow the Germans to occupy their country, the Germans were ready to fight their way in. Six naval task forces would land troops at Norway's major ports and the key airfields at Aalborg, Oslo and Stavanger would be taken by air assault, allowing follow-on ground units to be flown in. Supplies, heavy equipment and reinforcements would be brought in by three successive waves of cargo ships, transports and tankers. The Germans planned to put 10,000 troops ashore in Norway on the first day, accompanied by another 3,000 troops flown in. More than 100,000 troops were committed to the Norway operation.

German supply ship and a warehouse blazing fiercely, following the RAF's attack on Bergen harbour, April 1940. Norway was RAF Bomber Command's first real operation of World War II. Due to mediocre aircraft and poor training, Bomber Command inflicted relatively little damage on the German forces in Norway. (© Imperial War Museums, C 1254)

The Luftwaffe appointed Lieutenant Colonel Freiherr Carl August von Gablenz, a former senior manager of Lufthansa and one of the Luftwaffe's best air transport specialists, to oversee the air transport side of the operation. The air transport plan for *Weserübung* was crafted to get infantry reinforcements as well as essential support units such as engineers, signals troops, flak and airfield support units on the ground on the first day of the invasion. The Luftwaffe organized the transport force into nine large wings and consolidated many of the Luftwaffe's seaplanes and flying boats into a naval air transport wing. These aircraft did not need landing fields and could land directly in the harbours and fjords. During the campaign, these aircraft would play a vital role in airlifting troops and supplies to Bergen, Narvik and Trondheim.

German and Allied command and control

The Germans established functional headquarters and clear lines of command. The Kriegsmarine commander for *Weserübung* was Admiral Böhme, who created two regional naval commands: Norway West under Admiral Saalwächter and Norway East under Admiral Carls. The Luftwaffe commander was General Hans Geisler, commander of X Fliegerkorps. General Nikolaus von Falkenhorst was named theatre commander, although he only had authority over the army. However, his Gruppe XXI headquarters had naval and Luftwaffe liaison staffs. Although X Fliegerkorps was under the command of Luftwaffe headquarters, it was the norm in the Wehrmacht for Luftwaffe operational commands to co-locate with the army commands they were supporting, so any support requests or problems that came up could be immediately dealt with by face-to-face meetings with the commanders or chiefs of staff, who had the authority to make decisions and commit forces. As an army corps headquarters, Gruppe XXI staff had a Koluft (Luftwaffe commander) who served as direct liaison to the Luftwaffe. German corps and even divisions had specialist air liaison officers assigned with their own communications team. They ensured that the air corps was kept fully informed of the ground situation. The Luftwaffe committed more than 3,150 signals troops to *Weserübung* to ensure that all the services' headquarters were in close communication.

OPPOSITE NAVAL AND AIR MOVEMENTS 8–9 APRIL

The headquarters of the three service commands were all located in Hamburg at the start of the operation, where they had good communications facilities. The Luftwaffe and army headquarters were to relocate to Oslo several days after the invasion once good communications could be assured.

In planning for an intervention in Norway the British never set up a theatre headquarters. Plans were made to deploy naval and army forces to Narvik and, likely, to central Norway as well, with the main effort being Narvik. Each force was to report back to its service headquarters in London. At the strategic level there was the War Cabinet and under that was each service chief. Various committees could plan and coordinate but had no real authority. The British military, at this point in the war, functioned in a highly bureaucratic manner and it took time for each service to pass intelligence and information to the others. Each service was on its own, reporting back through its own channels to London.

Major General Pierse Mackesy, commander of the 49th Division, was named commander for the British Army's main intervention force (Avonmouth) to go to Narvik. But although he was to command a force that would grow to corps strength, he was given no staff to carry out the planning. With no operational-level headquarters or staffs set up, there was no plan for flowing troops or logistics into a combat theatre, no arrangements made for liaison teams with Norwegian forces, no plans for coordinating air support from the RAF or Royal Navy carriers with ground forces, and no plans to ensure interservice communications.

The intelligence picture

The Germans had military attachés in Norway, and the German planning staffs had good intelligence of the Norwegian military, coast and air defences. A great deal of effort went into putting reconnaissance planes over the North Sea to track British fleet movements. At the start of the war, the Germans had the advantage of superior signals intelligence. Two of the major code systems of the Royal Navy – the 'Naval Cypher' (for operational signals) and the 'Naval Code' (used for administration and ship movements) – had been largely broken by the Kriegsmarine's signal intelligence office, the 'B-Dienst'. By April 1940 German naval intelligence could read up to 50 per cent of the Naval Cypher, which provided the naval staff with accurate information about the locations and movements of the main Royal Navy fleet units.

In contrast, in early 1940 the British codebreakers had made little progress with the Kriegsmarine's Enigma codes. The Luftwaffe version of the Enigma code had been broken, but before the invasion German Luftwaffe and fleet units exercised radio silence. After the start of the invasion, Luftwaffe units relied mainly on radio communication, and the British Ultra programme was able to intercept and decrypt messages providing many Luftwaffe unit locations, organization and strength. However, even with good intelligence, the problem in early 1940 was the lack of good analysts who could sort through the raw data and identify the most important information, and a system to get intelligence quickly to the operational commanders who needed it. Thus, the codebreaking success that proved vitally important later in the war could not be exploited in the Norwegian campaign.

In summary, German plans and preparations for the campaign were thorough. There were enough forces and logistics so that when things went wrong the Germans could adapt. The Germans had a clear command and control system that enabled the services to operate together. In contrast, the British planning was abysmal, and the command and control system failed to coordinate the services. Poor planning and preparation, and the lack of interservice communication and cooperation, virtually doomed the British effort before the campaign had begun.

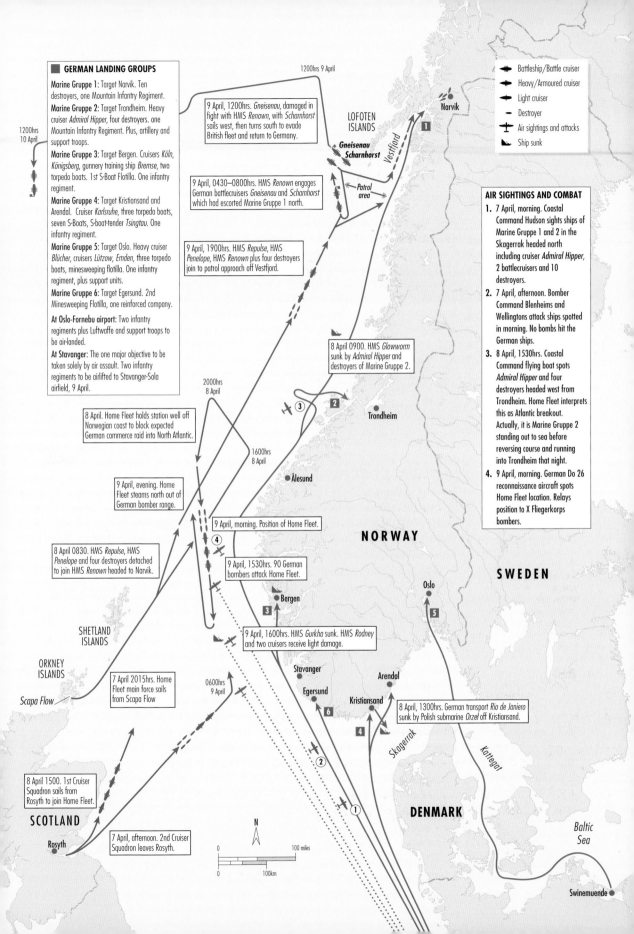

GERMAN LANDING GROUPS

Marine Gruppe 1: Target Narvik. Ten destroyers, one Mountain Infantry Regiment.

Marine Gruppe 2: Target Trondheim. Heavy cruiser *Admiral Hipper*, four destroyers. one Mountain Infantry Regiment. Plus, artillery and support troops.

Marine Gruppe 3: Target Bergen. Cruisers *Köln*, *Königsberg*, gunnery training ship *Bremse*, two torpedo boats. 1st S-Boat Flotilla. One infantry regiment.

Marine Gruppe 4: Target Kristiansand and Arendal. Cruiser *Karlsruhe*, three torpedo boats, seven S-Boats, S-boat-tender *Tsingtau*. One infantry regiment.

Marine Gruppe 5: Target Oslo. Heavy cruiser *Blücher*, cruisers *Lützow*, *Emden*, three torpedo boats, minesweeping flotilla. One infantry regiment, plus support units.

Marine Gruppe 6: Target Egersund. 2nd Minesweeping Flotilla, one reinforced company.

At Oslo-Fornebu airport: Two infantry regiments plus Luftwaffe and support troops to be air-landed.

At Stavanger: The one major objective to be taken solely by air assault. Two infantry regiments to be airlifted to Stavanger-Sola airfield, 9 April.

1200hrs 9 April

1200hrs 10 April

9 April, 1200hrs. *Gneisenau*, damaged in fight with HMS *Renown*, with *Scharnhorst* sails west, then turns south to evade British fleet and return to Germany.

LOFOTEN ISLANDS

Narvik

Gneisenau *Scharnhorst*

Vestfjord

Patrol area

9 April, 0430–0800hrs. HMS *Renown* engages German battlecruisers *Gneisenau* and *Scharnhorst* which had escorted Marine Gruppe 1 north.

9 April, 1900hrs. HMS *Repulse*, HMS *Penelope*, HMS *Renown* plus four destroyers join to patrol approach off Vestfjord.

8 April 0900. HMS *Glowworm* sunk by *Admiral Hipper* and destroyers of Marine Gruppe 2.

AIR SIGHTINGS AND COMBAT

1. 7 April, morning. Coastal Command Hudson sights ships of Marine Gruppe 1 and 2 in the Skagerrak headed north including cruiser *Admiral Hipper*, 2 battlecruisers and 10 destroyers.

2. 7 April, afternoon. Bomber Command Blenheims and Wellingtons attack ships spotted in morning. No bombs hit the German ships.

3. 8 April, 1530hrs. Coastal Command flying boat spots *Admiral Hipper* and four destroyers headed west from Trondheim. Home Fleet interprets this as Atlantic breakout. Actually, it is Marine Gruppe 2 standing out to sea before reversing course and running into Trondheim that night.

4. 9 April, morning. German Do 26 reconnaissance aircraft spots Home Fleet location. Relays position to X Fliegerkorps bombers.

2000hrs 8 April

8 April. Home Fleet holds station well off Norwegian coast to block expected German commerce raid into North Atlantic.

1600hrs 8 April

Trondheim

Ålesund

9 April, evening. Home Fleet steams north out of German bomber range.

9 April, morning. Position of Home Fleet.

8 April 0830. HMS *Repulse*, HMS *Penelope* and four destroyers detached to join HMS *Renown* headed to Narvik.

9 April, 1530hrs. 90 German bombers attack Home Fleet.

NORWAY

SWEDEN

SHETLAND ISLANDS

Bergen

9 April, 1600hrs. HMS *Gurkha* sunk. HMS *Rodney* and two cruisers receive light damage.

ORKNEY ISLANDS

Oslo

Stavanger

Arendal

Egersund

Kristiansand

Scapa Flow

7 April 2015hrs. Home Fleet main force sails from Scapa Flow

0600hrs 9 April

Skagerrak

8 April, 1300hrs. German transport *Rio de Janiero* sunk by Polish submarine *Orzeł* off Kristiansand.

Kattegat

8 April 1500. 1st Cruiser Squadron sails from Rosyth to join Home Fleet.

SCOTLAND

Rosyth

7 April, afternoon. 2nd Cruiser Squadron leaves Rosyth.

N

0 ——— 100 miles

0 ——— 100km

DENMARK

Baltic Sea

Swinemuende

Battleship/Battle cruiser
Heavy/Armoured cruiser
Light cruiser
Destroyer
Air sightings and attacks
Ship sunk

THE CAMPAIGN
The dawn of all-arms warfare

Flight of three Ju 52s over the town of Aalborg, Denmark, on the first day of the invasion. Overflights of Denmark on the first day of the invasion helped cow Danish resistance to the Germans. In fact, the Germans incurred only 20 casualties before Denmark surrendered on 9 April. (ullstein bild via Getty Images)

Germany's opening moves

A striking feature of the Norway campaign is the failure of the British to correctly assess numerous indications of the German force buildup and movements prior to 9 April. Through early 1940, RAF Bomber Command conducted a series of raids against German naval installations in the North Sea and reported on German dispositions. By early April, RAF reconnaissance showed that the Kriegsmarine was assembling shipping for a major operation. On 4 April agents' reports from Copenhagen warned of a German move on Norway. News of German shipping movements in the Baltic and Heligoland Bight was received on 6 April. The morning of 7 April a Coastal Command Hudson reported a German cruiser and six destroyers steaming north. The report took two and a half hours to get through headquarters bureaucracy and to the desk of Admiral Forbes, Home Fleet commander. At 1325hrs that day RAF Bomber Command spotted and attacked a Kriegsmarine squadron off the Skagerrak. The information was not passed on to the Home Fleet for four hours. Finally, that evening, Admiral Forbes realized that a German naval force was on the move and ordered the Home Fleet to sortie. On 8 April, a Royal Navy flying boat reported a German battlecruiser, two cruisers and two destroyers off the Norwegian coast steering west (actually, the heavy cruiser *Admiral Hipper* and four destroyers bound for Trondheim). Admiral Forbes was convinced that the Kriegsmarine would never try a major attack on Norway in the face of Royal Navy superiority. Instead, he believed that the movement of large German naval vessels meant that they were expected to turn west and break out north of Scotland and enter the North Atlantic to attack merchant shipping.

Forbes responded to the reports by sending out two parts of the Home Fleet on a northeasterly course to intercept a German breakout into the North Atlantic. This placed the British fleet well to the west of Norway and favoured the Germans as they moved north close to the coast. A further threat appeared to rob the Germans of surprise when, on 7 and 8 April, British destroyers and minelayers moved into Norwegian waters to mine the coastal shipping route used by the ore ships. In fact, the British hoped this action might

Mountain troops of the 3. Gebirgsjäger-Division disembarking in Trondheim the morning of 9 April. The German invasion forces at Bergen and Trondheim were very vulnerable in the first days after the landing before follow-on reinforcements and flak units arrived. The British had brigades ready for landings and considered an immediate counter-attack to seize Trondheim. Such a move was likely to succeed if done in the first days after the invasion. However, the British military chiefs failed to reach a decision and the opportunity passed as the Germans brought in reinforcements by air and strengthened their defences. (Author's collection)

lead to a friendly intervention of Allied forces to protect Norway. A British expeditionary force was already prepared to land at Stavanger after mining of Norwegian waters had been announced. On 8 April the British pulled back their light forces engaged in mining the Norwegian leads, but one of the last ships to leave the area, the British destroyer HMS *Glowworm*, encountered the heavy cruiser *Admiral Hipper*, which quickly sank the British destroyer. At 1530hrs on 8 April, a British patrol aircraft spotted the *Admiral Hipper*. But this served only to confirm the analysis that this was a commerce-raiding expedition into the Atlantic.

It seemed that the German attempt at surprise was blown on 8 April, when the German merchant ship *Rio de Janeiro*, bound for Bergen, was sunk by the Polish submarine *Orzeł* just off the Norwegian coast. German troops on board the transport were rescued by Norwegian naval and fishing craft. Their interrogation made it clear that the Germans were part of a force to land at Bergen the next morning. The Norwegian cabinet, holding an emergency meeting on 8 April, was informed and now knew an invasion was under way. Still hoping that negotiations with the Germans and the Allies might succeed, the Norwegian cabinet decided upon a cautious approach. Rather than call an immediate mobilization of the military (mostly reserve forces) by telephone and radio, the government opted for partial mobilization of selected units and to keep the orders quiet by sending them by post. Only the active military and coastal garrisons were put on alert. The Wehrmacht feared that the element of surprise had been lost, but the errors of the British High Command, Home Fleet and the Norwegian government made it possible for the Germans to still have a strong element of surprise when the attack began on 9 April.

The German attack on Denmark

The German planners for *Weserübung* saw that success depended on the immediate seizure of the Aalborg airfields located in northern Denmark. German fighters and Stukas required refuelling at an intermediate airfield before staging into southern

OPPOSITE
Admiral of the Fleet Sir Charles Forbes, Commander of the Home Fleet in 1940. Forbes was a traditional battleship admiral who had been at the Battle of Jutland and had commanded a cruiser in World War I. Forbes, who did not have a high regard for naval air power, sortied the main parts of his fleet against the Germans without carrier support on 9 April. Forbes would be relieved of command of the Home Fleet soon after the Norwegian campaign. (Photo12/ Universal Images Group via Getty Images)

OPPOSITE AIRBORNE OPERATIONS IN THE NORWAY CAMPAIGN

German soldiers occupy a Norwegian heavy coastal battery in the first days of the invasion. The Germans brought artillerymen in the first invasion wave to man the captured coastal defences and deter any British counter-landings. (ullstein bild via Getty Images)

Norway, and Aalborg was perfectly suited as a staging and refuelling point. The German 4. Kompanie of 1. Fallschirmjäger-Regiment was given two key missions in Denmark. One platoon of paratroopers would parachute directly onto the Aalborg West and East airfields at 0715. Its mission was to secure the airfields while a full infantry battalion was flown in. The other platoons of 4. Kompanie were to capture the Storstrøm Bridge that connected Falster Island with Zealand Island and hold it until the ground forces arrived. This two-span bridge was a key strategic point connecting the Danish islands, and one of the bridges was guarded by a small fortress, which, the Germans believed, might be manned.

The assault on Denmark that began at dawn on 9 April went according to plan. The fort near the Storstrøm Bridge was not manned, and 4. Kompanie took the bridge with no resistance. At Aalborg, the German platoon landed next to the main airfield, Aalborg West, and quickly captured the airfield intact. Once captured, Aalborg began to receive German aircraft, and within a day it became one of the major airfields of the Luftwaffe. During the next few weeks, Aalborg airfield would be a base for bomber and fighter forces. The Germans would build bunkers and fortifications and expand the airfield as it became a major Luftwaffe base.

The Kriegsmarine steams into Oslo

The German invasion of Norway on 9 April 1940 proves the old military axiom that no plan survives contact with the enemy. The German plan at Oslo was based on Hitler's optimistic prediction that the Norwegians would willingly accept a German invasion. Hitler insisted the landing at Oslo, Norway's capital, be treated as a *coup*

7. Narvik, May–June.
Facing an imminent attack by overwhelming Allied forces, Gen Dietl with less than 5,000 men in Narvik on 15 May requested a battalion of paratroopers be dropped. With no paratroopers immediately available following the Holland invasion, infantrymen of 137.Gebirgs-Regt with a short course in parachuting could be committed. Between 23–26 May, 218 of these soldiers were dropped in small runs of 3–4 aircraft. Between 26 May–2 June, 307 men of I./1.Fallschirmjäger-Regt were also successfully dropped to the Narvik garrison, which was forced to retreat to the Swedish border on 28 May when the Allies took the city. At least four transports carrying more than 50 soldiers were shot down or damaged on route and failed to drop their troops. The drops were good for morale and made for great propaganda, but their military effect was nil.

6. Hemnesöy, northern Norway, near Mo i Rana.
In a move to outflank the British/Norwegian defences near Mo i Rana the Germans dropped a platoon of paratroops from four Ju 52s to seize a blocking position at Hemnesöy on the Allied right flank. In the meantime, units of 2.Gebirgs-Div attacked in force on the Allied left flank. The operation was a success as it forced the Allies to abandon a strong defence position.

5. Dombas, central Norway, 14 April–19 April.
The town of Dombas was a key rail and road junction in central Norway that connected Oslo and Trondheim. In an airborne operation with virtually no planning or intelligence of the area or of Norwegian forces, 1./1.Fallschirmjäger-Regt (150 men) using 15 Ju 52s were dropped in bad weather over Dombas. One aircraft was shot down and crash-landed. Other aircraft missed their drop zones. The entire company was scattered in small groups within a 30km radius of Dombas, and many supply and weapons containers were lost in the darkness and snow. Over five days the paratroop bands, lacking food and ammunition, due to the failure of resupply drops, were tracked down and forced to surrender by the local Norwegian units.

4. Stavanger-Sola airfield, 0830hrs, 9 April.
Stavanger-Sola Airport was Norway's most modern airfield and was the strategic key to air superiority over southern Norway and the North Sea. At 0830 3./1.Fallschirmjäger-Regt (135 men) supported by Bf 110s from I./ZG 76 dropped at Stavanger-Sola airport, which was defended by two platoons of Norwegian Army troops. The paratroops secured the airfield by 0900hrs allowing two battalions of infantry to be flown in. Luftwaffe ground units were flown in and by evening squadrons of bombers, patrol aircraft, Stukas and fighters were stationed there.

3. Oslo-Fornebu airport, morning 9 April.
Oslo's main airport was to be taken by two companies, 1. and 2./1.Fallschirmjäger-Regt. With fog reported at Fornebu the mission was called off. But the second transport wave, carrying infantry of the 324th Regt, ignored the recall order and was joined by three of the Ju 52 transports with 50 of the paratroopers. Bf 110s of I./ZG strafed Fornebu, then, low on fuel, five landed under fire, and removed their rear machine guns to suppress the defenders. The transports with the second-wave infantry landed under fire and their soldiers secured the airfield for additional waves. By noon enough soldiers were on the ground to march a battalion into Oslo and seize the city.

1. Aalborg airfield, Denmark, dawn on 9 April.
A platoon of 4./1.Fallschirmjäger-Regt drops at 0700 at Aalborg airfield and seizes the airport in minutes. Luftwaffe units arrive and begin using Aalborg as a staging base.

2. Bridges in Denmark, 0500hrs, 9 April.
Three platoons of 4./1.Fallschirmjäger-Regt drop and secure Storstrøm Bridge connecting the island of Falster with Zealand to hold until motorized troops arrive. There is no Danish resistance.

German infantry disembark from a Ju 52 transport at Fornebu Airport on 9 April. Although German shipping was disrupted in the first days of the invasion, the Germans were able to flow in thousands of infantry soldiers and support units in the first week, allowing the Germans to rapidly secure southern Norway and Norway's major ports. (© Imperial War Museums, HU 50562)

de main rather than an invasion. Against the warnings of the Kriegsmarine leaders, Hitler insisted that Germany's newest heavy cruiser, *Blücher*, would lead Gruppe Five of the invasion force, navigate the long Oslo Fjord in the dark, and at dawn would be anchored before the capitol buildings of Norway. It was hoped that such a landing would so overawe the Norwegian government that the Germans could capture the country in one stroke.

However, when the German task force entered the Oslo Fjord at midnight on 9/10 April, it was challenged by guard boats, which the Germans fired on. Smaller German vessels landed at the Norwegian naval and seaplane base at Horten at the entrance to the fjord as the main ships of the task force proceeded to Oslo. Twenty kilometres south of Oslo the channel narrowed to 500m, and this was guarded by the Oscarsborg, an old fortress modernized in 1898–1901, with three 280mm heavy guns and a battery of torpedoes. The fort was minimally manned but had enough defenders to man the main batteries. At 0300 the heavy cruisers *Blücher* and *Lützow* were fired on at point-blank range. The *Lützow* was badly damaged and withdrew, but the *Blücher* took several critical hits. It would sink in the channel at 0700 with heavy loss of life. Later that day the Oscarsborg fortress was bombed by Ju 87s of StG 1, which damaged the fortress but did not compel surrender. The fortress only fell after a land attack.

The airborne attack at Fornebu Airport

With the main attack stopped, seizing Oslo now depended completely on the second part of the attack plan, the airborne assault upon Oslo's Fornebu Airport, located only 8km from the city centre. The plan was to have 1. and 2. Kompanien of 1. Fallschirmjäger-Regiment drop directly onto Fornebu Airport and seize the airport, allowing follow-on German transports carrying two infantry battalions and an engineer company from 324. Infanterie-Regiment to land and march into Oslo.

The German transport force ran into heavy fog as it approached Oslo at 0800. The plan specified that, in case of heavy fog, the airborne assault was to be called off. When the first transport wave carrying the paratroops received the recall order, it turned around to return to the newly seized Aalborg airfield. One transport crashed into the ocean and was lost, but three Ju 52s instead joined the second wave that carried the infantry to be air-landed after Fornebu was taken. General Geisler insisted that the air drop should not take place in heavy fog and that the second wave would also have to return. Lieutenant Colonel von Gablenz, commander of the land transport force, refused to recall his transport units, arguing that even without the paratroops, his transports could still seize the airfield. Geisler, believing the transports would be shot to pieces, sent out the recall order. However, the commander of the second transport formation proceeding to Fornebu, Captain Richard Wegner, ignored the abort order and suspected it might be a ruse since it had not come from his immediate chief, Lieutenant Colonel von Gablenz. Wegner was confident that the navigation skills of his pilots were good enough to find Fornebu, even in fog. Wegner was proved right; he found himself and his transport wave to be on course as the fog dissipated on the approach to Fornebu.

Norwegian Gladiators defend Oslo, 0730hrs, 9 April 1940

Norway's only modern fighter squadron consisted of ten Gloster Gladiator Mark IIs of the Norwegian Army Air Corps stationed at Oslo's Fornebu airfield. These were the last ten Gladiators built. Of the ten, the Air Corps mechanics could only make seven serviceable for action on the morning of 9 April, as three of the aircraft lacked spark plugs. It was just as well, as the squadron had only seven pilots fully qualified on the Gladiator. Alerted by the German attacks on the Norwegian guard ships at the mouth of Oslo Fjord at midnight, the Norwegians put up fighter patrols south of Oslo. A patrol of three fighters at 0600 found no hostile aircraft and landed at 0650. At 0700 a report of a large aircraft formation flying up Oslo Fjord was received, and all seven Gladiators attempted to take off, but one suffered engine failure and made an emergency landing.

Six Gladiators flew south at 5,500ft and soon encountered a German formation of 150 transports and escorting Bf 110s 30km south of Oslo flying at 3,200ft in an attempt to get under the heavy cloud cover.

In this scene, Norwegian Air Force First Lieutenant Dag Krohn, an experienced fighter pilot who had joined the air force in 1934, spotted three Ju 52 transports of KGr zbV 103 flying north at 3,200ft with a BF 110 of ZG 76 escorting them. The cloud cover hid his approach, and with a height advantage of 2,000ft Krohn was able to dive on the Bf 110 and shoot it down before he was spotted. Krohn was able to evade the other Bf 110 escort fighters by flying into the scattered clouds. The other Gladiators made a series of individual attacks on the German formation, shooting down another Bf 110 and a transport.

Afterwards, with Fornebu under attack, Lt. Krohn could not return to his base, so he and another Gladiator, piloted by Lt. Tradin, flew to a frozen lake near Oslo where they landed and, with the help of local people, refuelled their planes. The two Gladiators flew north and landed on frozen Lake Mjösa. However, the wheels of Tradin's aircraft broke through the ice and made it immobile. Lt. Krohn managed to take off again and fly his Gladiator to Hamar to join the remnants of the bomber squadron that had escaped from Sola-Stavanger airfield that morning. The other Gladiators of Norway's fighter squadron were not as lucky. One was shot down by a Bf 110 escort fighter. Another returned to Fornebu to refuel but was destroyed on the ground by German fighters. Two more Gladiators were damaged in the air battle south of Oslo and made emergency landings in fields near Oslo. Thus, by the afternoon of 9 April, Norway's total modern fighter force had been reduced to Lt. Krohn's Gladiator no. 421. At the end of the campaign in Norway, Lt. Krohn was able to escape to Sweden and eventually to the UK. He became a transport pilot for the RAF and served to the end of the war.

The Norwegian Air Force and the fight for Oslo

The main air defence for Norway's capital – indeed, the only modern fighter unit in all of Norway – was a squadron of ten Gloster Gladiator Mk II biplane fighters stationed at Fornebu. These ten aircraft were, in fact, the last Gladiators manufactured. The Norwegians, alerted by the night attack on the watch boats in Oslo Fjord, made seven Gladiators serviceable to fly at dawn on 9 April. The remaining three Gladiators were unflyable owing to a lack of spark plugs. At 0600 a patrol of three Gladiators took off and searched the area south of Fornebu and Oslo. Encountering nothing, they returned to the airfield 50 minutes later. At 0700, formations of enemy aircraft were reported to the south, and all seven Gladiators took off to intercept the Germans. South of Oslo, in the thick clouds, the second transport wave of Ju 52s, accompanied by He 111 bombers and a squadron of escorting Bf 110s from ZG 76, were encountered. Diving to the attack, the Norwegian pilots shot down two German transports. Two Bf 110 fighters were also shot down by the Gladiator biplanes, as they were much more manoeuvrable than the Bf 110s and could evade them in the clouds. The other Bf 110s drove off the Gladiators, damaging some of them. Unable to return to their base at Fornebu, now under attack by German fighters, the seven remaining Norwegian Gladiators, some severely damaged, made crash-landings around Oslo. Two Gladiator pilots, Lieutenant Krohn and Lieutenant Tradin, found a frozen lake at Tyrifjorden and safely landed their aircraft to refuel. Later that morning, Krohn and Tradin took off in their two aircraft and flew northwest. Landing upon another frozen lake, a wheel of Lt Tradin's Gladiator penetrated the ice and became trapped. Of Norway's only modern fighter squadron, only Lt Krohn's aircraft survived 9 April intact.

The attack on Oslo's Fornebu Airport was preceded by a squadron of long-range Bf 110 fighters led by First Lieutenant Werner Hansen. The Bf 110s strafed Fornebu airfield, destroying aircraft on the ground and suppressing the security units. Hansen's Bf 110s were in a desperate situation because they were operating at their maximum range and did not have enough fuel left to return either to Germany or even to recently seized Aalborg in Denmark. Seeing that the transports were ready to land, Hansen ordered his Bf 110s to land under fire after strafing the ground defences. Hansen's Bf 110s landed and taxied to the far end of the airfield, except for one Bf 110 which overshot the airfield and crashed. At the corner of the airfield, the Bf 110s' rear gunners were able to dismount their rear machine guns, and fired on the Fornebu defenders concentrated around the airport control tower and hangars.

The first transports carrying the infantry units now landed under fire from the ground. Two aircraft were destroyed and others heavily damaged. However, with the supporting fire of the grounded Bf 110 machine gunners, more transports landed and disgorged their infantry units, which formed up to attack the defenders. The Norwegian Army security units retreated, and soon a continuous stream of transports brought in infantry battalions, engineer units and Luftwaffe ground units to secure Fornebu Airport. By 1200 a German battalion had assembled and marched into Oslo to occupy the city. The Germans faced no resistance in Oslo, as the Norwegian government had evacuated the capital that morning and headed north to Hamar.

The Luftwaffe and the attacks on Kristiansand, Bergen and Trondheim

As at Oslo, German air power proved decisive in overcoming Norwegian defences at other locations on 9 April. At Kristiansand, the German invasion group could not enter the port at night due to heavy fog, and the group commander knew he would have to fight his way in. That morning he called for the Luftwaffe to bomb the coastal batteries protecting the port. Seven He 111s of KG 4 attacked, but the batteries remained in action. However, a second raid by He 111s of KG 26 at 0930 silenced the batteries of the two coastal forts and blew up

one of their ammunition magazines. After the air attacks an infantry landing party from the cruiser *Karlsruhe* and smaller naval craft captured the fortifications. By 1500 Kristiansand was in German hands with no further resistance.

Bergen was the objective of Group 3 with light cruisers *Köln* and *Königsberg* leading the landing force. Bergen was a difficult objective because it was the Norwegian city closest to the British coast, only eight hours' sailing time from the Home Fleet's main base at Scapa Flow. Thus, the Bergen force was the one most likely to be intercepted and targeted by British air and naval forces. The Group 3 commander sent landing parties in the early morning darkness to take the Norwegian defence batteries at Kvarven and German naval units passed into the fjord. However, other batteries were alerted and at 0515 the German landing party came under fire from Norwegian coastal batteries at Sandviken. The German supply ships *Brunse* and *Karl Peters* and the cruiser *Königsberg* all suffered heavy damage from Norwegian fire. But the naval group managed to move past the coast defence batteries and land troops in the harbour at 0630. The city fell without resistance, but coastal batteries at Kvarven and Sandviken held out until the bombers of KG 4 carried out an intensive aerial bombardment at 0700 which was followed up by a German infantry attack. Once Bergen fell to German hands, KGr zbV 108 (Transport Group 108) airlifted 159. Infanterie-Regiment there using Ju 52s modified as seaplanes. Without a good airport, Bergen harbour became the main landing field for the Germans.

Trondheim was a key objective of the campaign – first because it dominated central Norway, and second, Værnes airfield lay just outside the city. The German invasion group of four destroyers and the cruiser *Admiral Hipper* arrived at the entrance to Trondheim Fjord at 0300 on 9 April and proceeded past the coastal batteries at the fjord entrance. Troops landed

Oslo on the afternoon of 9 April 1940. A German infantry battalion marches the 6km from the Fornebu airfield to Oslo city centre unopposed, as five years of German occupation of Norway begins. (Universal History Archive/UIG via Getty Images)

A bomb from an aircraft of the Coastal Command falls on Ju 52 transport seaplanes of KGr zbV 108 moored in Bergen harbour, 1940. Coastal Command carried out numerous attacks on German ports and shipping in Norway but inflicted little damage. (© Imperial War Museums, C 1194)

from destroyers seized the Norwegian coastal fortifications. The *Admiral Hipper* and one destroyer anchored at Trondheim and German infantry from the 138th Mountain Regiment secured the city without resistance at dawn.

Værnes airfield near Trondheim was no more than a grass field built in 1936, and the April weather turned the field into a bog, unusable for transport aircraft. The Luftwaffe, however, used the Kü Fl Gr (Coastal Aviation Group) 506 equipped with He 115 seaplanes. Although most He 115s carried out their usual task of long-range reconnaissance that day, on 9 April, 14 He 115s ferried in troops and supplies, landing directly on the fjord at Trondheim's harbour.

Seizing Stavanger airfield by airborne attack

Sola airfield, just outside Stavanger, was a major strategic target for the Germans on the first day of the invasion. The Sola airfield was the most modern airfield in Norway, as it possessed a concrete runway, rather than the grass runways of most European airfields of the 1930s. The large transport and bomber aircraft now being produced were too heavy for old-fashioned grass airfields, so concrete runways were being built throughout Europe. The concrete runway at Stavanger would enable all-weather operations for transports and bombers. In addition, a seaplane harbour and ramp was located on the inlet next to the airfield, so seaplanes and flying boat units could be co-located with land-based aircraft. Most importantly, Stavanger's position located on the southwestern tip of Norway made it the best strategic position to control the airspace over the North

Sea and central Norway. From Stavanger it was only 500km to the British naval bases. Holding Stavanger was central to both German and Allied plans for fighting in Norway. While British planning had emphasized Narvik, it also noted the importance of putting forces and aircraft into Stavanger.

The Germans employed 3. Kompanie of 1. Fallschirmjäger-Battalion in the operation. The Norwegian Army had an infantry battalion stationed only 5km away. With the warnings that came on the night of 8 April, preparations were made to defend the airfield. The Norwegian 8th Infantry Regiment deployed two platoons with 64 soldiers to guard the airfield. Some defence bunkers were under construction, but as of 9 April, only one bunker had been completed. The two platoons had a few old machine guns for airfield defence, but no heavy anti-aircraft weapons.

The German attack on Stavanger was preceded by Bf 110s that strafed the field and destroyed two aircraft of the Norwegian Air Force squadron stationed there. Seven of the nine obsolete bombers stationed at Stavanger took off earlier in the morning for airfields in eastern Norway. The attack was initiated at 0830, and the Bf 110s were able to suppress most Norwegian defensive fire. Just after the fighter strafing, 12 Ju 52s dropped a company

Fallschirmjäger take Stavanger-Sola airfield, 9 April 1940

9 April 1940 saw the first use of a radical new method of warfare – airborne assault. On the first day of the Norway campaign the Germans counted on paratroops to seize four key strategic objectives: Aalborg airfield in Denmark, the Storstrøm Bridge in Denmark, Fornebu Airport at Oslo and Sola airfield at Stavanger. Stavanger was Norway's most modern airfield, an all-weather, concrete-surfaced airfield located at the tip of Norway's southwestern coast. If the Germans occupied Sola airfield, their bombers could dominate the air over southern Norway and the North Sea.

Armed only with pistols and hand grenades, German paratroopers normally dropped from low altitude (300ft) to get on the ground quickly. Rifles, MP 38 submachine guns, machine guns, mortars and ammunition were dropped in special containers. On landing, the paratroop platoons would assemble, gather the weapons containers, and arm themselves, then move on the objective. The assault on Stavanger-Sola would be the first test of paratroops in taking a defended objective.

Stavanger-Sola airfield was defended by a detachment of 64 Norwegian infantrymen from the 8th Infantry Regiment deployed to the airfield that night. There is also a detachment of Norwegian Air Force ground crew assigned to the Norwegian Air Force squadron stationed there. The Norwegians were building nine bunkers for airfield defence, but only one bunker, located a few hundred metres north of the runway, had been completed.

Eight Bf 110Ds of I./ZG 76 were assigned to support the paratroop attack on Stavanger-Sola, but four aircraft aborted the mission when encountering heavy fog. Two aircraft collided en route and had to ditch. So, only two Bf 110s arrived to support the airborne assault, but these were enough to effectively suppress most of the Norwegian defenders. The defenders' only anti-aircraft weapons were some obsolete machine guns that overheated and jammed. The only effective Norwegian resistance was the one completed bunker north of the runway that was able to lay heavy fire on many of the landing paratroops.

This scene shows Stavanger-Sola airfield east of the main runway at 0830hrs, 9 April. A total of 110 paratroopers of the Luftwaffe's 3. Kompanie, 1. Fallschirmjäger-Regiment have just landed with the objective of seizing the airfield. The paratroopers in the foreground include a 2nd Lieutenant (with binoculars) and a sergeant next to him (rank is denoted by badges on the upper arm of their left sleeves), and soldiers are forming around their officer and sergeant. Four paratroopers have just recovered their weapons container and are joining the group in the foreground, looking to the north end of the airfield where the Norwegian bunker has a machine gun that has pinned down part of the paratroop company. One of the supporting Bf 110s is seen in the background strafing the airfield buildings where most of the Norwegian defenders were concentrated.

Although the paratroops of 3. Kompanie took as many as 30 casualties, some paratroopers managed to move behind the bunker and silence it. With effective resistance ended, the Norwegian infantry detachment retreated and by 0900 the paratroopers were in full control of the airfield, capturing 40 Norwegian Air Force ground personnel. More than 200 Ju 52 transports carrying troops of 193. Infanterie-Regiment and Luftwaffe airfield units began arriving.

That afternoon Bf 110 fighters and Ju 87 Stukas arrived at Stavanger-Sola to be ready for operations against the Royal Navy. He 115 reconnaissance planes were stationed at the seaplane base next to the airfield. Bomber units would soon arrive, and within three days Stavanger-Sola became one of the Luftwaffe's main bases for the Norway campaign. The success of the paratroop operations in Denmark and at Stavanger was the first use of paratroops in warfare and dramatically demonstrated the effectiveness of the concept.

Flight of Ju 52 transports over the North Sea in the first wave of the German invasion, morning of 9 April 1940. More than 500 Ju 52 transports were employed from 9 April until early May, when most were redeployed to northern Germany to support the spring offensive in the West. The Luftwaffe's transport force played a decisive role in the Norway campaign, transporting 29,000 troops by air from Germany to Norway, along with 2,000 tons of equipment and supplies. (Author's collection)

of 110 paratroopers on the airfield. One defence bunker put many paratroopers under fire as they dropped. But some paratroopers landed outside the bunker's field of fire and assembled, collected weapons from drop containers and disabled the bunker.

By 0900 Stavanger airfield was in German hands, and the next wave of 200 Ju 52s arrived, bringing two battalions of 193. Infanterie-Regiment. Air-landed infantry occupied the town of Stavanger, only 6km distant, without any further resistance. The transports then flew in Luftwaffe ground airfield units and flak units. By evening, bombers, a squadron of Bf 110s and a squadron of Stukas were all deployed to Stavanger and these forces would grow quickly. Reconnaissance He 115s took over the seaplane base. Luftwaffe logistics was helped by the capture of 67 tons of aviation fuel stored at Stavanger. In the first week of *Weserübung*, a large part of X Fliegerkorps' combat and reconnaissance aircraft was stationed there.

The first British responses
The Narvik landings and the Home Fleet's intervention

Narvik was far out of range of German airfields, so that it was the only landing on 9 April that did not receive any Luftwaffe air support. At Narvik, a flotilla of ten of Germany's newest-model destroyers landed a regiment and support troops, approximately 2,500 men, from the elite 3. Gebirgs-Division (3rd Mountain Division) directly at the port of Narvik. Two old Norwegian coast defence ships resisted and were quickly sunk. After that, the local garrison commander, an associate of Norway's pro-Nazi former War Minister Vidkun Quisling, surrendered the port without resistance. However, to the northeast of Narvik, up on the Norwegian-Soviet border, the Norwegian 6th Division with 8,000 men had been mobilized since the beginning of the Russo-Finnish War in October 1939, and its commander, Major General Carl Fleischer, quickly reoriented much of his division to move south to resist the German landings at Narvik.

The German commanders knew well that the most dangerous opponent of the entire operation was the Royal Navy. Thus, General Geisler kept a large part of his bomber force in reserve at airfields on the north German coast, ready to intervene against any sorties by the Royal Navy. The Luftwaffe's reconnaissance priority was to monitor the Royal Navy, and on 9 April X Fliegerkorps flew 49 sorties over the North Sea to track the Home Fleet.

The Home Fleet, having been warned about German naval activity by its reconnaissance, was already at sea on 9 April in two strong detachments. The Home Fleet, with four battleships, three heavy cruisers, seven light cruisers and 14 destroyers, under the direct

The port of Narvik seen from the air, April 1940. For both Germans and the Allies, Narvik was the focus of the Norway campaign due to its strategic iron-ore port. (© Imperial War Museums, HU 104687)

command of Admiral Forbes, was stationed at sea 150km off Bergen. A second naval group from the Home Fleet, made up of four light cruisers and seven destroyers, under Admiral Leyton, was northwest of Forbes' position. Both detachments were stationed well out at sea, in expectation that the Kriegsmarine's heavy vessels would try a breakout into the North Atlantic and begin commerce raiding.

Admiral Forbes had taken a major part of the Home Fleet out to sea without air cover. Only one carrier, HMS *Furious*, was available to the Home Fleet in early April. On that day it was docked in the Clyde for a refit and a day's sailing away from the Home Fleet squadrons. Two other carriers might have been available to the Home Fleet, but both HMS *Glorious* and the Royal Navy's most modern carrier *Ark Royal* had been sent to the Mediterranean for exercises. This was surprising, for at this point in the war, the Mediterranean remained peaceful and Italy would not enter the war until 10 June 1940. Forbes apparently had so little regard for carrier air power that he felt comfortable sailing his fleet without it.

The British main force under Admiral Forbes was spotted by a reconnaissance group of KG 30's Ju 88 bombers, which arrived over the fleet at 1530. It was soon joined by a group of Ju 88s and a group of KG 26's He 111s, a total of 90 bombers. The Luftwaffe bombers began a relentless attack that lasted until dark. The Heinkels of KG 26 reported that they had made three hits each on two British battleships, and reported additional hits on a battle cruiser, a heavy cruiser and two troops ships. KG 30's Ju 88s claimed hits on two battleships, a heavy cruiser and a cruiser. As is typical for bomber operations, the battle damage assessment was way off the mark. Despite reports of massive damage, only one ship was sunk, the destroyer HMS *Gurkha*, and the cruisers *Devonshire*, *Glasgow* and *Southampton* suffered only minor damage from near misses. As for the report that troopships had been sunk, there were no troopships with the British fleet. However, the battleship *Rodney* was hit by a 500kg bomb that failed to explode. For the relatively small damage inflicted on the British fleet, the Germans had lost four Ju 88 bombers. Yet, the encounter had been a shock to the British. In one afternoon's action, the Home Fleet had fired 40 per cent of its anti-aircraft ammunition, and after the repeated but generally unsuccessful bombing attacks, Forbes moved his vessels away from the coast, out of range of German bombers.

The next day, Forbes moved his force north to rendezvous with the carrier HMS *Furious*. However, *Furious* would not be an asset to cover the fleet because, during its refit at the Clyde, its squadrons of Skua fighter/dive bombers had been put ashore and were now stationed at the Hatston Naval Air Station near Scapa Flow. This meant *Furious* could not provide any fighter cover for the fleet if attacked. It had sailed only with its venerable Swordfish biplane torpedo bombers aboard.

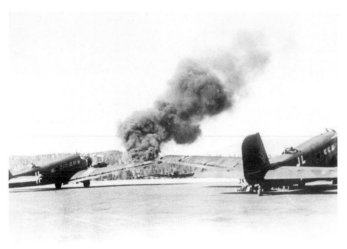

Troops unloading at Oslo-Fornebu Airport, 9 April 1940. A crashed Ju 52, lost in the morning attack, burns in the distance. Although the paratroop landing at Fornebu was cancelled, the airport was taken by the decision of the transport commander to land transports carrying infantry under fire. (© Imperial War Museums, HU 93725)

The evening of 9 April Forbes informed the Admiralty that it would be impossible for major fleet units to operate near the Norwegian coast because of German air superiority. Any interdiction of German vessels returning from the invasion forces would have to be carried out by the British submarines.

The Royal Navy strikes back

While the Germans could claim victory on 9 April, when all their key objectives were met, the next days would witness some retribution from the Royal Navy. Narvik, over 1,500km from Germany, had always been the Germans' most difficult objective. At Narvik, the Germans lacked reconnaissance aircraft and air cover to keep them informed of the Royal Navy's movement. Moreover, U-boats that had been dispatched to the waters around Narvik to look for the British encountered bad weather and failed to spot British activity.

The British already had several naval task forces at sea in the Norwegian theatre. Nearby was the Royal Navy's Second Destroyer Flotilla, which had been a part of a force laying mines in Norwegian waters. The ten German destroyers at Narvik had planned to get away quickly but they required refuelling, and the single German tanker that reached Narvik could only fuel two destroyers at a time. There was a day's delay in readying the German destroyers to retreat to Germany. It proved disastrous. At dawn on 10 April British flotilla commander, Captain Warburton-Lee, took his five destroyers into the fjord unobserved by U-boats nearby. The British flotilla achieved full surprise against the German destroyers in Narvik harbour. With torpedoes and gunfire, the British quickly sank two German destroyers and damaged three more. However, as they exited Narvik harbour on their return to the Norwegian Sea, five German destroyers stationed in flanking fjords attacked Warburton-Lee's force. In a sharp engagement, two British destroyers were sunk and another damaged.

Learning the fate of Warburton-Lee's flotilla, the British rushed a task force consisting of the battleship HMS *Warspite* and nine destroyers to Narvik. This time, the British had the reconnaissance advantage. Using the reconnaissance floatplane on the *Warspite*, The British task force was able to note the locations of all the German destroyers. On 13 April, the British task force attacked the remaining German destroyers. Against the massive firepower of the *Warspite*'s 15in guns, the destroyers had little chance. Destroyers damaged in the first battle of Narvik were quickly sunk, and one was beached. The remaining five German destroyers retreated to the far end of the Rombaksfjord. One destroyer, attempting a torpedo attack against the British, was quickly sunk. After firing their torpedoes and most of their ammunition, the four remaining German destroyers deliberately beached themselves so that their crews could escape. Having destroyed all ten of the German destroyers – half of Germany's destroyer fleet – the British task force withdrew to the mouth of the fjord while the British commander signalled the Royal Navy that Narvik was theirs for the taking.

The German Army force at Narvik, under the command of Generalleutnant Eduard Dietl, was now stranded, far from any hope of easy German resupply or reinforcement. Some 1,900 sailors of the Kriegsmarine had survived the two sea battles, so Dietl organized them into naval battalions. Luckily for the Germans, the nearby Norwegian Army depot held more than 8,000 rifles and 324 machine guns, as well as Norwegian Army winter clothing. So, Dietl could equip and organize his 1,900 sailors, who had undergone only rudimentary training in army weaponry, into naval battalions that could be used to reinforce his regiment of elite mountain troops. Dietl had 4,400 men armed largely with commandeered weapons, as well as a few weapons salvaged from Germany's wrecked ships. With this small force, far from Germany, he would have to face the full onslaught of the British.

While six German landings had been successful and the Germans controlled all of Norway's major cities, the intended *coup de main* had failed. The sinking of the *Blücher* afforded the Norwegian government sufficient time to evacuate the King and cabinet to the town of Hamar, then on to Elverum, only 80km from the Swedish border. Back in Berlin, Hitler believed that Vidkun Quisling, the pro-Nazi former war minister, might set up his own government – a political blunder of the first order. Quisling immediately stepped into the political vacuum in Oslo and attempted to assemble his own cabinet and government. Curt Bräuer, the German ambassador to Norway, had expected Norway's legitimate government to seek an armistice with the German invaders. He held that Norway would accept German military occupation if it allowed for Norwegian local government and sovereignty, the same arrangement the Germans had negotiated with the Danes. However, the attempt of Quisling to form a Norwegian government without the consent of either the King or the 'Great Assembly', the Stortinget,

Major General Otto Ruge, named commander-in-chief of the Norwegian armed forces on 10 April 1940. Ruge performed very credibly, mustering more than 40,000 Norwegian troops to fight the Germans. But Ruge was hampered by poor communications with his units. He attempted to work with the British commanders, but the British commanders failed to provide effective support or cooperation with the Norwegians. (Bettmann/Getty Images)

outraged the Norwegian government and it refused a Quisling government outright. Nor did it see any reason to enter negotiations with the Germans, foreseeing that a major Allied counter-attack was imminent. The Germans belatedly realized their blunder. Ultimately, Quisling and his puppet government failed to get German recognition. Instead, a German official, Josef Terboven, was placed in power by Hitler on 19 April 1940, assuming the role of Norway's civil government administrator.

The quick seizure of Norway's major urban areas made it difficult for the reserve-based Norwegian Army to mobilize. Most of Norway's population lived along the coasts, so that the inland areas were sparsely populated. German detachments occupied the towns along the fjords before the Norwegian government's mobilization orders could arrive by mail. Norwegians ordered to mobilize found their towns and reserve depots already in German hands. Thus, no more than 40,000 of the 106,000-man Norwegian Army ever mobilized to fight the Germans. The Norwegian forces in southern Norway retreated inland, away from the Germans, and in the first days of the Norway campaign they remained in a state of disorder owing to the poor communications of the Norwegian military.

The old and ineffectual Norwegian military chief General Kristian Laake was removed on 10 April and replaced with the more energetic Colonel Otto Ruge, immediately promoted to major general. General Ruge began organizing Norwegian defences against the German advance inland. Ruge recognized that, owing to Norway's mountainous interior terrain, the German advance was limited to two possible routes that followed the rail lines into central Norway. Trondheim, located 500km from Oslo, was the key to central Norway and Ruge's top priority was to move the government inland and defend Gudbrandsdal, which contained the major rail line from Oslo to Trondheim. Completed only in 1920, the Oslo–Trondheim rail line that traversed Norway's interior mountains had been a difficult feat of engineering. With Trondheim cut off by the Royal Navy, it was now an isolated island for the Germans and far removed from the main German forces now holding southern Norway. Ruge believed with British help he could have enough forces to block the rail line at Gudbrandsdal and check the German advance. A British landing at Trondheim or central Norway would enable the British to link with the Norwegians and keep hold in central Norway.

Taken by surprise, the Royal Navy organized immediate strikes on the German forces before they had time to consolidate their defences. Early on the morning of 10 April, the

Blackburn Skua squadrons of HMS *Furious*, based on land at Royal Naval Air Station Hatston near Scapa Flow, took off to attack German ships at Bergen. The cruiser *Königsberg*, which had been damaged by Norwegian coastal batteries the day before, was tied to the dock in Bergen and had been unable to make a quick return to Germany. Flying more than 400km from their base with 500lb bombs, the Skuas were at the absolute maximum of their range. The Germans had little time to set up a flak defence in Bergen harbour. With only its own anti-aircraft guns for defence, the *Königsberg* was an easy target. Arriving at 0805, the Skuas tipped into their shallow 60-degree dive and quickly struck the *Königsberg* with three 500lb bombs, with several near misses. The bombs turned the *Königsberg* into a burning wreck and it capsized in minutes. The Skua had made naval history by being the first aircraft to sink a major warship by dive bombing. The 15 Skuas arrived back at Hatston with bone-dry fuel tanks.

By 11 April, Admiral Forbes' task force of three battleships, three heavy cruisers, and 18 destroyers had finally joined with the carrier *Furious*, which, lacking its Skua fighters, carried only its Swordfish torpedo-bomber squadrons. Forbes set course for Trondheim and at 0400 launched the *Furious*'s 18 Swordfish torpedo-bomber biplanes. Unlike the raid at Bergen, the British air raid on Trondheim was a complete failure. The best target, the German cruiser *Admiral Hipper*, had already left Trondheim with one destroyer on 10 April to return to Germany, but their absence and movement had been missed by Home Fleet reconnaissance. However, there were still three German destroyers in Trondheim harbour and the Swordfish attacked them. All the torpedo attacks failed, owing to the shallow depth of the harbour.

Blenheim I bomber. The Blenheim, with a three-man crew, entered service in 1937 as a light bomber. For the time, it was fairly fast (265mph max speed) but carried only a 500kg bombload and two machine guns. The lack of a de-icing system made the Blenheim ineffective in operations over the North Sea. It was obsolete as a bomber in 1940 but served effectively as a night fighter in 1941 and 1942. (Popperfoto via Getty Images)

On 11 April Bomber Command made its first raid against German forces in Norway by sending six Wellington bombers and two Blenheim light bombers to strike the Germans at Værnes airfield near Trondheim. Værnes was essentially inoperable due to heavy rainfall and resulting slush. So, the first raid by the RAF Bomber Command did little damage.

The main problem for the air strikes against the Germans in Norway was not German resistance, as the Germans had only limited anti-aircraft defences at this time. The main problem was the spring weather over the North Sea, which was highly changeable and often featured persistent low cloud cover as well as extreme low temperatures. In such conditions, heavy icing on the aircraft surfaces, especially the wings, occurred readily, causing the losses of several RAF aircraft. The poor weather also taxed the RAF's limited capabilities for navigating long distances over open sea. At this point in the war, the British lacked not only navigational experience but also the navigational aids that they would employ very effectively later in the war. Despite extensive efforts to try to find and attack German warships and supply ships at sea, the Royal Air Force managed to sink only a single German supply vessel. Furthermore, the RAF's bombing offensive against Germans in the Norwegian theatre was problematic because the aircraft of Bomber Command at this time were limited by their light bombloads and their range, which put most Norwegian targets at extreme range.

The British submarine offensive

On 1 April 1940, Vice Admiral Max Horton, commander of the Home Fleet's submarine force, ordered every available submarine of his force to stations off the Norwegian coast by 8 April. Horton was the only senior British commander to expect that, as a matter of course, there would be a strong German naval response to the Royal Navy's plan to mine the 'Leads', the inshore waters off Norway's west coast. So, 18 British submarines, including the Polish submarine *Orzeł* operating under British command, were in patrol position off the

The pilots and flight crews of No. 50 Squadron Bomber Command at the RAF Waddington airfield pose with one of their Hampden bombers after a raid on German shipping off Bergen on 11 April 1940. (H.F. Davis/PNA Rota/Getty Images)

Ju 52 transport lands on frozen lake at Trondheim, the cargo moved by horse-drawn sledge. Owing to the poor condition of Værnes airfield, during April the Luftwaffe used a frozen lake for both transports and bombers as Vaernes airfield was rebuilt with a hard runway. (© Imperial War Museums, HU 94380)

Norwegian coast as the German invasion began. On 8 April two German cargo ships, the *Rio de Janeiro* and the fleet tanker *Posidonia*, were sunk by British submarines. The next day, the British submarines tore into the cargo ships and tankers, bringing the second wave of troops into Norway. Four German merchant vessels were sunk by submarines and a further one lost to a mine laid by a submarine. Between 8 and 14 April, British submarines accounted for 13 tankers or troopships either bringing the second wave and third waves of German supply and reinforcement or returning from the first wave. In addition, British submarines inflicted heavy losses on the Kriegsmarine's warships as they tried to return to Germany after landing the invasion force. On 9 April, the cruiser *Karlsruhe* was sunk, and on the 11th, the cruiser *Lützow* was badly damaged. On 14 April, the *Brummer* gunnery training ship was sunk by a British submarine.

Aggressive action by the British submarine force, soon augmented by two French submarines, threw Hitler and the OKW into something of a panic. The follow-on reinforcements and supplies for the German invasion had been badly disrupted. Not just supplies were lost. On 10 April, the troopship *Friedenau* was torpedoed, and 384 soldiers from 340. Infanterie-Regiment were lost. The British submarines decimated the next wave of merchant ships detailed to resupply the German forces in Bergen, Trondheim and Stavanger. Even shipping to Oslo was threatened. If the Royal Navy could stop resupply by sea then the whole operation would be in jeopardy. The forces in Trondheim were in danger of being cut off and forced to surrender. In this crisis, OKW called a meeting of army and navy transport chiefs to devise a plan to resupply and reinforce forces in Norway with light, fast vessels, less vulnerable to submarines than large merchant ships, and to run most supplies and reinforcements the short distance from northern Denmark to the southern Norwegian ports of Oslo and Larvik. As these ports became the primary German logistics bases, less vulnerable light vessels would move troops and supplies along the coast to Stavanger and Bergen. In the meantime, the Kriegsmarine organized an anti-submarine defence line from Denmark to the Skagerrak, behind which the heavy merchant ships could safely sail. The Kriegsmarine proved the fast transport concept by shipping a full army battalion in S-boats from Stavanger to Bergen on 15 April with no losses. The convoys of light vessels from Denmark to Norway started on 16 April and proved an immediate success.

German counter-submarine operations paid off. In April three British submarines were sunk by German naval action. On 5 May, the submarine HMS *Seal* was damaged, forced to the surface and captured. In early June, the Polish submarine *Orzeł* that had initiated the submarine offensive with the sinking of the *Rio de Janeiro* on 8 April, was sunk. The losses of Admiral Horton's submarines could not be sustained. In May, most of the Home Fleet's submarine force was redirected towards the Dutch coast when the German spring offensive began. Finally, the Germans were able to restore ship convoys to Bergen and Trondheim.

However, before the German counter-submarine campaign took effect, the German garrisons in Bergen, Trondheim and Narvik were cut off from sea supply until May. Concerned with the situation at Trondheim, OKW ordered the navy to help supply the Luftwaffe at Værnes airfield and the Kriegsmarine detached four U-boats to carry ammunition, and especially aviation fuel, to supply Trondheim.

OKW also had to contend with the erratic leadership of the Führer. When the destroyers were all lost at Narvik and the mountain troops were stranded there, Hitler had, as General Jodl put it, 'a case of nerves' and wanted to order Generalleutnant Dietl to retreat south, which was impossible in the roadless, mountainous Arctic terrain. Another day, Hitler wanted the force to be airlifted out – another impossible task as Narvik was without an airfield. In the end, Jodl calmed Hitler by an effort to resupply and reinforce the Narvik force by air. During April and May, ammunition, priority equipment, and even light artillery pieces and reinforcements, were flown to Narvik, mostly by seaplanes and flying boats that landed in the fjord. The improvised airlift, which included supply drops by parachute, and reinforcement by a few companies of mountain troops given hasty parachute training and airdropped on Narvik, brought Generalleutnant Dietl 1,000 troops as well as supplies. Because of this airlift, Dietl was able to hold Narvik and tie down a large Allied/Norwegian force for two months.

RAF Bomber Command operations over Norway

Britain's immediate response to the German landings relied on naval and air power. As well as sending detachments of the Home Fleet to sea, RAF Bomber Command was ordered to disrupt the German air and naval operations. Beginning on 9–10 April, Bomber Command sent out small raids, usually six to 12 aircraft, at first striking German naval forces and shipping off Norway. The first attack, on 9 April, included 24 Hampden bombers searching for warships off Bergen and eight Blenheims carrying out reconnaissance patrols.

Norwegian ports and airfields at Stavanger, Trondheim and Oslo were chosen as key targets, along with the airfields at Aalborg. The RAF's intent was to disrupt German shipping and reinforcement and to cripple the Luftwaffe's key bases in Norway. The RAF learned of the difficulties of carrying out long-distance operations in the Norwegian theatre. Most Bomber Command aircraft, especially the Whitleys and the Hampdens, had only light defensive protection. Unlike the Germans, who had the Bf 110 long-range escort fighter, the RAF had no fighters capable of escorting bombers on long-range missions. British bombers, with their light defensive armament and without fighter escorts, were expected to penetrate well-defended German airspace in Norway. The Luftwaffe had rushed numerous flak units, both light and heavy, to defend its new key bases in Norway, and Bf 110 fighters and Me109s defended the bases at Stavanger and Aalborg. Already handicapped by their mostly obsolescent, lightly armed aircraft, the British also now faced an effective flak and fighter defence.

Handley Page Hampden medium bomber. The Hampden was in service with ten RAF squadrons in 1940. It had a 250mph maximum speed, a range of 1,760km and carried a maximum bombload of 1,800kg. The Hampden was already obsolescent in 1940 and was nicknamed the 'flying suitcase' because conditions for its four-man crew were so cramped. By 1941, it was taken out of active operations. (The Print Collector via Getty Images)

The first raids were carried out in daytime, but the British learned some very harsh lessons early on. On 12 April, a major mission was put together to attack shipping at Stavanger. RAF Bomber Command deployed 83 aircraft against Stavanger, with 36 Wellingtons, 24 Hampdens and 23 Blenheims. In the daylight raid, the RAF bombers met intensive flak and fighter opposition; six Hampden and three Wellington bombers were lost. This operation was the largest offensive bombing operation of the RAF to date. The minimal damage to German shipping, resulting in more than 10 per cent losses for the British, pushed Bomber Command to transition to night operations for future raids. However, the aircraft were ill-equipped for such missions and the pilots poorly trained to fly at night and in bad weather, so that generally they were ineffective. Between 9 April and 10 May, when the German invasion in the West forced the RAF's attention to divert to the battle for France, most nights saw a small effort, with handfuls of British bombers sent out to attack shipping and airfields. Only a small portion of Bomber Command was ever employed in the one-month RAF bombing campaign in the fight for Norway. Bomber Command reports noted that almost half of all the sorties of the Bomber Command over Norway were either aborted in flight owing to bad weather, or saw entire flights and squadrons of the RAF unable to find the target and bomb effectively.

The RAF bombing campaign was not helped by the lack of intelligence. It should have been obvious from the start that the airfields at Aalborg were essential to the German effort, and disabling those airfields would result in serious difficulties for the Germans. Yet Aalborg was first bombed only 11 days into the campaign, when, on the night of 20/21 April, a few aircraft attacked. The next night 12 Wellingtons were sent to bomb Stavanger and Aalborg airfields, and for four days small numbers of RAF bombers were sent to bomb Aalborg, which was so packed with aircraft that RAF reconnaissance pilots reported 'aircraft parked wingtip to wingtip'. However, most Luftwaffe aircraft used Aalborg West airfield, and the RAF mistakenly bombed Aalborg East nearby, which held only a few German aircraft.

During the month of Bomber Command's operations against the Germans in Norway, there were 268 daylight bombing sorties and 663 night sorties flown. From 9 April to 10 May 1940, Bomber Command dropped only 198 tons of bombs on the Germans in Norway and Denmark. In addition to the bombing effort, dozens of minelaying missions had been flown at night. For the small number of bombs dropped, Bomber Command lost 36 aircraft destroyed and others written off as irreparably damaged. The Wellingtons had proved to be Bomber Command's most effective aircraft of the time. It was clear that Blenheim light bombers were already obsolescent in the European theatre. The performance of the Whitleys and Hampdens was so mediocre that RAF Bomber Command determined to pull them from operations as soon as possible.

Reorganizing the Luftwaffe command

While providing a good operational command centre for the thousand-plus Luftwaffe aircraft committed to Norway, in the first days of the campaign it was clear that the Luftwaffe effort needed to be reorganized. On 12 April, the Luftwaffe decreed the formation of Luftflotte 5 as the higher command responsible for Norway. General Erhard Milch, the State Secretary for Aviation, assumed command. X Fliegerkorps under General Geisler remained as the operational headquarters for the flying units. While normally Luftwaffe air fleets had two or more air corps under its command, X Fliegerkorps was almost double the size of a standard Luftwaffe air corps. The Luftflotte 5 headquarters took over responsibility for the Luftwaffe support and logistics units and most Luftwaffe ground forces, to include the flak units, a large part of the Luftwaffe's force structure. Milch immediately announced the creation of two Luftgau (air district) headquarters to serve as command and control for the Luftwaffe's support, administrative, airfield engineer and flak units. Milch also ordered the establishment of Luftpark (Air Depot) Oslo, to be manned by 200 civilian mechanics and technicians of the Luftwaffe. The Luftpark would serve as a central repair and maintenance centre for the Luftflotte and also oversee the transfer of replacement aircraft and aircrew to the forward units.

General Milch had proved himself a capable senior manager since his days as a director of Lufthansa. As state secretary for aviation, Milch had been responsible for actually running the Luftwaffe, overseeing training, building, procurement and aircraft development in the

Armstrong Whitworth Whitley medium bomber. The Whitley entered service in 1937 as a night bomber and equipped eight squadrons of RAF Bomber Command. It had a range of 2,650km and carried up to 3,000kg of bombs. However, it was slow (230mph max speed) and obsolescent. (The Print Collector via Getty Images)

General Erhard Milch speaking to pilots of StG 1 (Sturzkampfgeschwader 1) at Værnes airfield in Trondheim in April 1940. As commander of Luftflotte 5, Milch reorganized X Fliegerkorps bombers, dive bombers, fighters and reconnaissance aircraft into air task forces to focus on different missions. Milch also ensured timely and effective logistics support for the air units committed to Norway. It was Milch's first, and only, opportunity to serve as a field commander and his performance as Luftwaffe commander in Norway from 12 April to 10 May was very good. (Photo by Heinrich Hoffmann/ullstein bild via Getty Images)

rapidly expanding Luftwaffe. Milch put his management skills to work. X Fliegerkorps did not have a large enough staff to manage what had become a large and complex logistics operation, so it made sense to leave the operational flying to the Fliegerkorps and leave the support and logistics to the Luftflotte. The Luftflotte 5 headquarters was established in Hamburg, near Falkenhorst's Gruppe XXI headquarters, because communications facilities were better in Hamburg. Both headquarters were moved to Oslo a week later once adequate communications had been set up. Creation of Luftflotte 5 and Milch's appointment ensured that priorities were given to providing strong flak defences for Luftwaffe airfields and that logistics for combat units would flow more efficiently.

Milch immediately set up a new command, a Luftwaffe version of the operationally oriented all-arms battle group that the army routinely used. Fliegerführer Stavanger (Air Task Force Stavanger) was set up with Colonel Robert Fuchs, commander of KG 26, as its head. As Stavanger was now the primary Luftwaffe base for the Norway campaign, 190 aircraft were placed under Colonel Fuchs, to be used for several missions: anti-shipping operations over the North Sea, fighter defence for southern Norway, and supporting the army in southern and central Norway. Stavanger became the main operational base for bomber and long-range fighter units and most of the Stukas (StG 1) for the next month.

Air power in the battle for central Norway: 9 April to 3 May
Trondheim: the key for both sides
Only days into the German invasion, it was clear to Hitler and the OKW that, while they had successfully taken their initial objectives, the Norwegians were not going to accept an armistice on the Danish model. With British intervention expected at any moment,

it looked like a long campaign had begun and the Wehrmacht needed to wrap up the operations in central Norway quickly to allow most of the Luftwaffe units in Norway to be returned to Germany to participate in the spring offensive. The German Army and Luftwaffe had only three weeks to drive the Allied forces out of central Norway before a large part of the air support was taken away.

While the populous south of Norway was being rapidly occupied, the hold on Narvik and Trondheim remained tenuous. Generalleutnant Dietl's force of approximately 4,400 men was in the worst position as it was cut off by the Royal Navy, had no airfield, and only a few of the Luftwaffe's transport aircraft had the range to airdrop supplies.

An He 111 bomber, snowbound on a Norwegian airfield, likely Trondheim. Weather in Norway in late winter/ early spring shut down air operations for days at a time and cost Allied and German air forces numerous operational losses from accidents. (Author's collection)

Trondheim's invasion force was only 2,000 men, and it was cut off from receiving supplies or reinforcements by sea. Because of the British submarine offensive, only one of three supply ships in the second wave made it to Trondheim. Two tankers sent to Trondheim were also lost. In April–June the Germans lost 21 merchant ships of 111,700 gross register tons in Norwegian waters. Owing to the poor state of Værnes airfield at Trondheim, it was difficult to supply and reinforce Trondheim by air. Trondheim was vulnerable to being taken – if the British moved quickly enough.

Trondheim, located 500km by road or rail from Oslo, was the obvious target for any Allied counterstrike. One of Norway's largest cities, it was the key to controlling central Norway. It was linked by rail not only to Oslo in the south, but also to Bergen in the southwest, and the lines extended 200km into the north as well. If Trondheim were taken by the British, they could easily pour in military forces and even advance to Bergen and Oslo with the help of the Norwegian forces. If Trondheim fell to the Allies, there would be no hope for the Narvik garrison, because Værnes airfield could control the airspace of central Norway to Narvik and cut off any aerial resupply. Conversely, if the Germans could hold Trondheim and use its airfield to full effect to win air superiority, neither Allied armies nor Allied navies could survive in central Norway.

Working with the Luftwaffe, von Falkenhorst prioritized the reinforcement of the German force in Trondheim. Using airlift, partly with seaplanes and flying boats landing on Trondheim Fjord, the Germans quickly lifted in troops and equipment. By 13 April, two batteries of anti-aircraft guns had been flown in as well as a battery of medium artillery. On the 14th, seven Stukas were detailed to operate out of Værnes airfield, even though the airfield was scarcely usable owing to snow and mud. That same day, an additional infantry battalion was flown in. The Kriegsmarine detailed four U-boats to run the British blockade and bring aviation fuel and ammunition to the Trondheim force. By 21 April, the Germans had built their force in Trondheim up to 5,000 men. This left the Germans with a strong force to guard Trondheim and 2,500 troops, including artillery and engineers, to mount an offensive against the British approaching from Namsos.

Since the grass airstrip at Værnes was unusable on most days in April, Luftflotte 5 decided to use a frozen lake, Jonsvatnet, only a few kilometres from Trondheim centre, as an airfield. While Værnes airfield was being rebuilt by Luftwaffe engineers and hired local Norwegians, the Luftwaffe flew hundreds of transport sorties to land on the frozen lake. But as the Germans had already learned from their experience at Narvik, frozen lakes in the Norwegian late winter were not ideal airbases. Starting on 17 April, the problems of using a frozen lake

Ju 88 being refuelled and serviced, Norway, April 1940. General Milch ensured a robust logistics and repair system was in place for Luftflotte 5 when it was formed so that a high tempo of operations could be maintained. (Author's collection)

became evident when, during one of the rapid thaws and overnight freezes characteristic of late winter in Norway, the wheels of a Ju 88 from KG 4 sank into the ice and froze. The aircraft was quickly locked so deeply in the ice that not even heavy equipment could pull the plane free. It was stripped of instruments, weapons and parts and left derelict. Between 17 and 21 April, the same fate befell three Ju 88s and one He 111. All four aircraft eventually sank into the lake.

Rebuilding Værnes airfield with a hard runway so that it could safely accept heavy aircraft and operate in all weather conditions required improvisation. The Germans hired hundreds of Norwegian labourers to cut and emplace heavy wooden beams for use as a hard runway surface. The Germans were able to recruit willing Norwegian labourers owing to the vastly different style of occupation policy Germany imposed on Norway from that imposed upon the Poles during their occupation in 1939. According to Hitler's racial theories, the Nordic Danish and Norwegian peoples were considered racially superior to the Slavic Poles or Russians, so in Norway 1940 there would be no ruthless style of forced labour and abuse of the population that was the norm in Poland. Of course, all of that would come to Norway later, but in April 1940, German troops were under strict orders to treat the Norwegians with every consideration, hoping to win them as allies of the greater German Reich. The Germans offered Norwegian workers good wages and extra food, tobacco and alcohol rations to rebuild Værnes airfield – one that would be used against their own Norwegian forces. Yet the Germans found few problems recruiting labour. A Norwegian worker later explained his motivation: 'During the 1930s Norway was a poor country, and my family was very poor, and the Norwegian government had done nothing to help us. Then the Germans came and offered good wages and extra rations, and we took the opportunity to work for them.'

The work of rebuilding Værnes airfield proceeded quickly, and by the end of April an 800m wooden runway was in operation. The Germans could move heavy bombers and Bf 110 fighters to Værnes, and Ju 87s were now within short range of the British bases at Åndalsnes and Namsos and could fly multiple missions per day with full bombloads. Placing

Heavy British anti-aircraft gun defending the Allied base at Harstad. British anti-aircraft units did not begin to arrive until the end of April as the Allies set up Harstad as their main base of operations against Narvik. The shortage of anti-aircraft guns made the Allied bases highly vulnerable to German bombing. (Keystone-France/Gamma-Rapho via Getty Images)

bombers at Værnes also put the Germans several hundred kilometres closer to the British forces at Narvik. While still a long distance from Trondheim, German bombers could now stage out of Værnes and attack the British main base at Harstad.

The naval raid on Stavanger

Seeking a means to cripple the Germans' rapidly growing air power in southern Norway, the Royal Navy on 17 April sent the heavy cruiser HMS *Suffolk* along with four destroyers to make a nighttime surprise attack on Sola Stavanger airfield, which lay on a peninsula directly on the coast. The British hoped a heavy barrage by naval guns would destroy a large number of aircraft at Stavanger and cripple the base. In the pre-dawn darkness, British seaplanes dropped flares to illuminate the airfield to enable gunfire spotting. But radio problems made the spotting less effective. The only major damage from the one-hour bombardment was to the nearby seaplane base, where four He 115s were destroyed and several other aircraft damaged. As the *Suffolk* escaped with the dawn, the Germans mounted a day-long series of air attacks on the task force that included more than 60 bomber sorties. The *Suffolk* took direct hits from two bombs and arrived back at Scapa Flow sinking, with water literally coming over its deck. The *Suffolk* would require major repairs and could not return to service until February 1941.

The Germans look to central Norway

Within three days of the invasion, German ground units, being continuously reinforced through Oslo, pushed out to occupy southern Norway. Columns pushed north from Oslo in pursuit of the Norwegian government, which had fled 70km north to Hamar on 9 April. The main Norwegian Army unit was the 2nd Division, which had only partially mobilized. This division, along with a smattering of other units, retreated northwest towards the centre of the country. The Norwegian Army's lack of a modern signals system meant that the army's new commander, Major General Otto Ruge, was out of contact with most of his

Henschel Hs 126, a high-wing monoplane carrying a pilot and an observer that proved a capable, rugged aircraft that could fly from small, primitive airfields. The Hs 126 was the standard short-range reconnaissance aircraft of the Luftwaffe for providing the army with both observer and artillery-spotting support. (Author's collection)

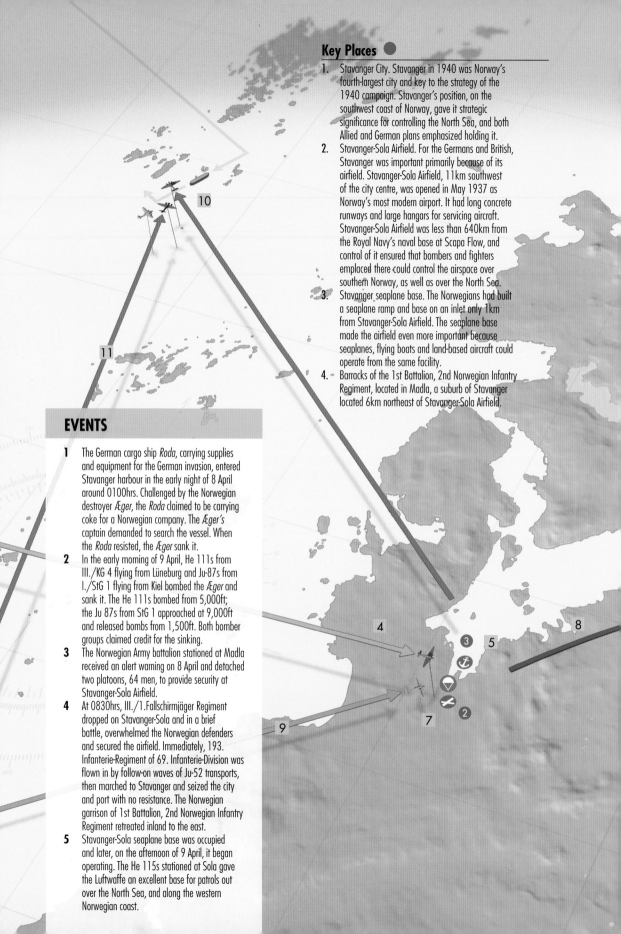

Key Places ●

1. Stavanger City. Stavanger in 1940 was Norway's fourth-largest city and key to the strategy of the 1940 campaign. Stavanger's position, on the southwest coast of Norway, gave it strategic significance for controlling the North Sea, and both Allied and German plans emphasized holding it.

2. Stavanger-Sola Airfield. For the Germans and British, Stavanger was important primarily because of its airfield. Stavanger-Sola Airfield, 11km southwest of the city centre, was opened in May 1937 as Norway's most modern airport. It had long concrete runways and large hangars for servicing aircraft. Stavanger-Sola Airfield was less than 640km from the Royal Navy's naval base at Scapa Flow, and control of it ensured that bombers and fighters emplaced there could control the airspace over southern Norway, as well as over the North Sea.

3. Stavanger seaplane base. The Norwegians had built a seaplane ramp and base on an inlet only 1km from Stavanger-Sola Airfield. The seaplane base made the airfield even more important because seaplanes, flying boats and land-based aircraft could operate from the same facility.

4. Barracks of the 1st Battalion, 2nd Norwegian Infantry Regiment, located in Madla, a suburb of Stavanger located 6km northeast of Stavanger-Sola Airfield.

EVENTS

1. The German cargo ship *Roda*, carrying supplies and equipment for the German invasion, entered Stavanger harbour in the early night of 8 April around 0100hrs. Challenged by the Norwegian destroyer *Æger*, the *Roda* claimed to be carrying coke for a Norwegian company. The *Æger's* captain demanded to search the vessel. When the *Roda* resisted, the *Æger* sank it.

2. In the early morning of 9 April, He 111s from III./KG 4 flying from Lüneburg and Ju-87s from I./StG 1 flying from Kiel bombed the *Æger* and sank it. The He 111s bombed from 5,000ft; the Ju 87s from StG 1 approached at 9,000ft and released bombs from 1,500ft. Both bomber groups claimed credit for the sinking.

3. The Norwegian Army battalion stationed at Madla received an alert warning on 8 April and detached two platoons, 64 men, to provide security at Stavanger-Sola Airfield.

4. At 0830hrs, III./1.Fallschirmjäger Regiment dropped on Stavanger-Sola and in a brief battle, overwhelmed the Norwegian defenders and secured the airfield. Immediately, 193. Infanterie-Regiment of 69. Infanterie-Division was flown in by follow-on waves of Ju-52 transports, then marched to Stavanger and seized the city and port with no resistance. The Norwegian garrison of 1st Battalion, 2nd Norwegian Infantry Regiment retreated inland to the east.

5. Stavanger-Sola seaplane base was occupied and later, on the afternoon of 9 April, it began operating. The He 115s stationed at Sola gave the Luftwaffe an excellent base for patrols out over the North Sea, and along the western Norwegian coast.

The seizure of Stavanger

KEY

✈ **Airfield**

⚓ **Seaplane base**

★ **Barracks**

▽ **Airborne assault**

STAVANGER

EVENTS

6 In support of *Weserübung*, in the afternoon of 9 April, three cargo ships of the sea transport echelon as well as one German tanker arrived in Stavanger Harbour. The ships carried heavy equipment, vehicles, artillery, and ammunition to supply the 69. Infanterie-Division. Stavanger was the one major Norwegian port occupied not by naval landing, but solely by an air-landing operation. This allowed the German transports to bring in the troops, who were then married up with their equipment that arrived by sea. As the 69. Division arrived by air over the next days, columns were quickly formed and moved out over land to connect up with the German landing forces at Bergen to the north and Kristiansand to the east.

7 On the first day of the invasion, Stavanger-Sola became a major German airbase. One squadron of Ju 87s, a squadron of Bf 110 fighters, and a reconnaissance squadron were all based at Stavanger by the evening of the 9th. One squadron of bombers also arrived on 9 April, and more bombers, including a squadron from KG 26, arrived over the next few days. The German air units began immediate operations covering the North Sea. The quick and efficient seizure of Sola airfield yielded 67 tons of Norwegian aviation fuel, enabling the Germans to begin immediate operations.

8 Troops of the 193. Infanterie-Regiment advance from Stavanger-Sola Airfield to Stavanger city, which falls early afternoon of 9 April without resistance.

9 From 11 April to 8 May, RAF Bomber Command made Stavanger the major focus of its Norwegian bombing operations. RAF Bomber Command carried out 22 raids against Stavanger -Sola. Most of the raids were small affairs with fewer than ten aircraft. The first RAF raid on 11 April was by six Wellingtons. Only three dropped bombs, and one was lost to the defending fighters.

10 17 April, 0515hrs. Royal Navy cruiser HMS *Suffolk* with four escorting destroyers approached Stavanger-Sola Airfield from the north and fired a barrage of 202 8in shells from 15km for one hour. At 0615hrs HMS *Suffolk* retired to the northwest, and headed for Scapa Flow. At 0830hrs KG 26 bombers from Stavanger-Sola spotted HMS *Suffolk* and began air attacks from 10,000ft. KG 30 Ju 88s from Westerland (Sylt) arrived at 1035hrs and made effective attacks, diving to 2,000ft before releasing bombs.

11 HMS *Suffolk* is severely damaged by the German bombers which pressed attacks into the afternoon (60-plus bomber sorties flown from KG 26 and KG 30, although almost half were unable to find the target) and the *Suffolk* is only saved by a squadron of Blenheims that arrived to cover the ship and fend off the Ju 88 attacks.

units. A coordinated counter-offensive was impossible, but with the units at hand Ruge could establish a defensive position in central Norway and hope for a British landing. If the British could take Trondheim, then they could link up with the Norwegians by rail and pour in troops and supplies.

The mountainous centre of Norway offered only two routes for the Germans to advance the 500km from Oslo to Trondheim. The best route was the Gudbrandsdal, which followed the rail line through the mountains to Trondheim and Åndalsnes. The other route, farther to the east, was the Østerdal, which had a road through Norway's central mountains, and which linked up to the road and rail lines to Trondheim near the Dombås rail junction. Both valleys contained narrow passes that made for excellent defensive positions. In the first week after the invasion, the Norwegian forces retreated to block the entrances to Gudbrandsdal and Østerdal and hold out until British help arrived.

The German fiasco at Dombås

Hitler, nervous about the setbacks at Narvik and fearful that a British landing might destroy the isolated force at Trondheim, insisted that the paratroopers carry out a mission deep behind Norwegian lines to prevent a linkup of British forces with the main Norwegian forces. The site selected for an airdrop was the key rail and road junction at Dombås, almost 400km from Oslo and 200km from the front lines of the advancing Gruppe XXI forces. Against the advice of the Army and Luftwaffe, OKW ordered an airborne operation for 14 April. With almost no planning, little intelligence and virtually no reconnaissance due to bad weather, 185 men of 1. Kompanie, 1. Fallschirmjäger-Battalion dropped in early evening around Dombås. Flying in sleet and low clouds, aircraft became lost and the paratroopers were dropped in small groups over an area of 30km. Most of the paratroop platoons landed 10 or more kilometres from their drop zones. Many of the weapons and supply containers were dropped in the dark and never recovered. Later supply drops failed to reach the paratroopers, now short of weapons, ammunition, and food. Of 15 Ju 52s used, one aircraft was shot down and seven more crashed due to lack of fuel or were forced to make emergency landings. Only seven planes returned to Oslo. During the next five days the small bands of paratroopers were hunted down by the Norwegian forces and forced to surrender.

Gruppe XXI offensive in central Norway

While reinforcing their forces in southern Norway, Gruppe XXI formed two large battle groups to advance into central Norway. The main effort was under Generalleutnant Richard Pellengahr, commander of 196. Infanterie-Division, formed around 324. and 345. Infanterie-Regimente supported by artillery, engineers, motorized machine-gun units and a detachment of tanks. Gruppe Pellengahr would advance down the main rail line through the Gudbrandsdal. The second battle group under Colonel Fischer was organized around 340. Infanterie-Regiment and had tank, artillery, and engineer support. Group Fischer would advance down the Østerdal Valley towards Trondheim. General Milch had stationed most of KG 4 at Oslo-Fornebu with its primary task to support the army's advance. A squadron of ten Hs 126 aircraft was also stationed at Oslo with the mission of providing reconnaissance and artillery spotting for the army. Per doctrine, specially trained Luftwaffe liaison teams with their own communications teams were assigned to the Gruppe XXI headquarters to help coordinate air support. When weather permitted, the army would enjoy a generous degree of air support.

General Ruge had no more than 7,000 soldiers and three batteries of 75mm guns under his direct command to hold the German advance. He was outnumbered, heavily outgunned and short of ammunition and supplies. He had no anti-tank guns. He also had no air support.

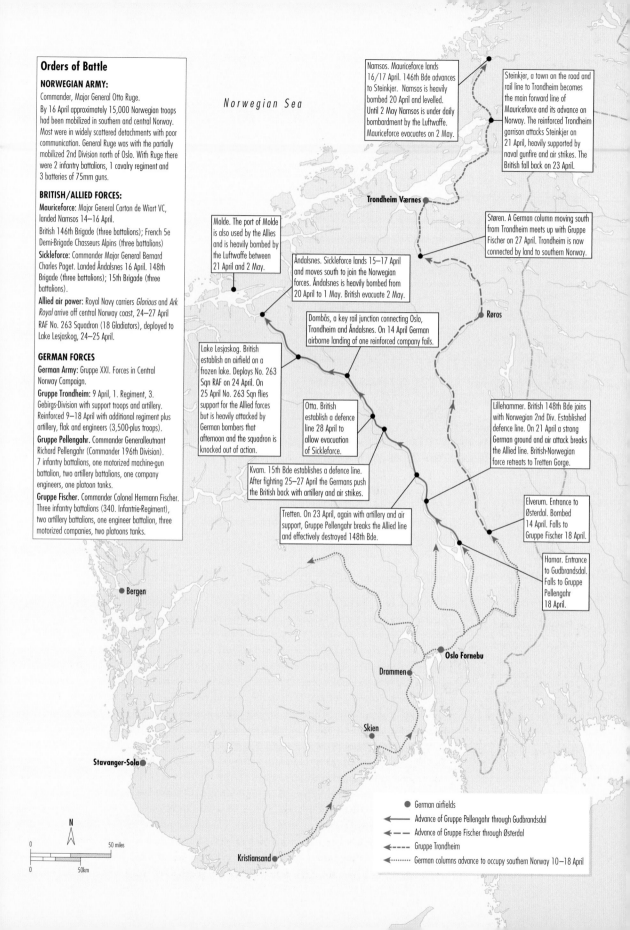

Orders of Battle

NORWEGIAN ARMY:

Commander, Major General Otto Ruge.

By 16 April approximately 15,000 Norwegian troops had been mobilized in southern and central Norway. Most were in widely scattered detachments with poor communication. General Ruge was with the partially mobilized 2nd Division north of Oslo. With Ruge there were 2 infantry battalions, 1 cavalry regiment and 3 batteries of 75mm guns.

BRITISH/ALLIED FORCES:

Mauriceforce: Major General Carton de Wiart VC, landed Namsos 14–16 April.

British 146th Brigade (three battalions); French 5e Demi-Brigade Chasseurs Alpins (three battalions)

Sickleforce: Commander Major General Bernard Charles Paget. Landed Åndalsnes 16 April. 148th Brigade (three battalions); 15th Brigade (three battalions).

Allied air power: Royal Navy carriers *Glorious* and *Ark Royal* arrive off central Norway coast, 24–27 April RAF No. 263 Squadron (18 Gladiators), deployed to Lake Lesjaskog, 24–25 April.

GERMAN FORCES

German Army: Gruppe XXI. Forces in Central Norway Campaign.

Gruppe Trondheim: 9 April, 1. Regiment, 3. Gebirgs-Division with support troops and artillery. Reinforced 9–18 April with additional regiment plus artillery, flak and engineers (3,500-plus troops).

Gruppe Pellengahr. Commander Generalleutnant Richard Pellengahr (Commander 196th Division). 7 infantry battalions, one motorized machine-gun battalion, two artillery battalions, one company engineers, one platoon tanks.

Gruppe Fischer. Commander Colonel Hermann Fischer. Three infantry battalions (340. Infantrie-Regiment), two artillery battalions, one engineer battalion, three motorized companies, two platoons tanks.

Norwegian Sea

Namsos. Mauriceforce lands 16/17 April. 146th Bde advances to Steinkjer. Namsos is heavily bombed 20 April and levelled. Until 2 May Namsos is under daily bombardment by the Luftwaffe. Mauriceforce evacuates on 2 May.

Steinkjer, a town on the road and rail line to Trondheim becomes the main forward line of Mauriceforce and its advance on Norway. The reinforced Trondheim garrison attacks Steinkjer on 21 April, heavily supported by naval gunfire and air strikes. The British fall back on 23 April.

Trondheim Værnes

Støren. A German column moving south from Trondheim meets up with Gruppe Fischer on 27 April. Trondheim is now connected by land to southern Norway.

Molde. The port of Molde is also used by the Allies and is heavily bombed by the Luftwaffe between 21 April and 2 May.

Åndalsnes. Sickleforce lands 15–17 April and moves south to join the Norwegian forces. Åndalsnes is heavily bombed from 20 April to 1 May. British evacuate 2 May.

Røros

Dombås, a key rail junction connecting Oslo, Trondheim and Åndalsnes. On 14 April German airborne landing of one reinforced company fails.

Lake Lesjaskog. British establish an airfield on a frozen lake. Deploys No. 263 Sqn RAF on 24 April. On 25 April No. 263 Sqn flies support for the Allied forces but is heavily attacked by German bombers that afternoon and the squadron is knocked out of action.

Otta. British establish a defence line 28 April to allow evacuation of Sickleforce.

Lillehammer. British 148th Bde joins with Norwegian 2nd Div. Established defence line. On 21 April a strong German ground and air attack breaks the Allied line. British-Norwegian force retreats to Tretten Gorge.

Kvam. 15th Bde establishes a defence line. After fighting 25–27 April the Germans push the British back with artillery and air strikes.

Tretten. On 23 April, again with artillery and air support, Gruppe Pellengahr breaks the Allied line and effectively destroyed 148th Bde.

Elverum. Entrance to Østerdal. Bombed 14 April. Falls to Gruppe Fischer 18 April.

Hamar. Entrance to Gudbrandsdal. Falls to Gruppe Pellengahr 18 April.

Bergen

Oslo Fornebu

Drammen

Skien

Stavanger-Sola

Kristiansand

N

0 — 50 miles

0 — 50km

● German airfields

← Advance of Gruppe Pellengahr through Gudbrandsdal

←--- Advance of Gruppe Fischer through Østerdal

←---- Gruppe Trondheim

←······· German columns advance to occupy southern Norway 10–18 April

German troops on the train from Oslo to Trondheim. The main German advance in central Norway followed the 500km train line from Oslo to Trondheim, to the Gudbrandsdal. Because British submarine action cut off supply by ship to Trondheim, opening the land and rail link from Oslo became the major objective of the German ground campaign in April. (ullstein bild via Getty Images)

However, he had some hope because the British had landed at Åndalsnes and Namsos, and a British brigade was rushing down by rail to join his forces at Lillehammer, at the entrance to Gudbrandsdal. It would be the first direct clash of the British and German armies in World War II.

The Allies land in central Norway

In the first four days after the German invasion of Norway, Britain's War Cabinet, the three service chiefs, and the Joint Plans Committee had held several meetings to decide a strategy. British intelligence on German forces in Norway was vague. The debate went back and forth as to whether Narvik would be the main priority for a British counterstrike, or Trondheim. In the end, no clear resolution for the campaign priority was ever set by the British service chiefs. The British service chiefs refused to appoint a theatre commander, so all the forces deployed to Norway reported back to their own service headquarters in London. The naval and army forces allocated for the Narvik counter-offensive were placed under a separate commander, Admiral Lord Cork, and not under the command of the Home Fleet. Each army expedition had its own separate commander. No headquarters or single commander had an explicit responsibility for coordinating what became three separate operations. It was war by committee and very bureaucratic.

The British had already planned to move units to Norway weeks before, when military intervention was discussed in the Cabinet. However, little had been done to train, equip, or prepare the brigades selected for Norway. The newly formed 24th Brigade consisted of three regular battalions, none of which had trained or worked together. The new brigade commander had never seen some of the units in his brigade and did not meet some battalion commanders until deployed to combat. The 146th Brigade of the 49th Territorial Division had been selected early in the planning process. Territorial divisions had few regular officers and their training level was low. On 10 April, the French government committed one division of the *chasseurs alpins* (mountain troops), 15,000 men, to the Norway operation and they were already assembling at Brest. The expedition to Narvik saw its orders changed three times in four days, guaranteeing almost total confusion for the British forces.

Namsos and Åndalsnes

The 24th and 146th Brigades set off for Narvik on 12 April. En route, on the 14th, the convoy commander was ordered to divert the 146th Brigade to the small Norwegian port of

German soldiers arriving at Stavanger's Sola airfield, 12 April 1940. (ullstein bild via Getty Images)

Namsos, 195km from Trondheim. The British service chiefs decided against a direct strike on Trondheim in preference to landing one force north of Trondheim and one force south of Trondheim, and both would move to cut off the German garrison. For fear of German air power, both forces would be landed a considerable distance from Trondheim. The southern landing would be 160km south of Trondheim at the small port of Åndalsnes. The two forces (Namsos had the codename 'Mauriceforce', and Åndalsnes 'Sickleforce') would be sent British and French reinforcements as soon as a base was established. Namsos harbour was secured by the Royal Navy, and 146th Brigade landed on 15 April. Major General Adrian Carton de Wiart had been named commander of Mauriceforce for only two days before flying to Namsos aboard a Coastal Command Sunderland flying boat on 15 April. De Wiart was a commander with no headquarters staff, no communications troops, no aides, and had to improvise an ad hoc headquarters from some officers that he quickly rounded up. The large transports carrying his troops landed more than 100km north of Namsos to be farther out of sight and range of the Luftwaffe. Troops would be ferried to Namsos aboard destroyers and the small trawlers of the Royal Navy. Without a proper port facility, unloading supplies and equipment and transshipping was a slow process and artillery and ammunition was mislaid in transit. General de Wiart found himself with infantry, but few signallers, no artillery and no anti-aircraft guns.

Åndalsnes was occupied by Royal Marines on 17 April followed by 148th Brigade, commanded by Brigadier General Harold Morgan. The 148th Brigade was already understrength, having only two instead of the usual three battalions, and it lacked heavy weapons. Fast cruisers and destroyers brought the troops ashore, and General Morgan contacted the Norwegians to assess the situation. The Norwegians, facing a strong German force ready to move west through the Gudbrandsdal, requested immediate support from British troops. General Morgan changed the plan from moving on Trondheim from the south to diverting his force to central Norway to help the Norwegians. This decision essentially killed the strategy of cutting off Trondheim and gave the German force there more time to fly in reinforcements. Åndalsnes was connected to the main Trondheim–Oslo rail line by a branch line; on 18–19 April two companies of the 5th Leicestershire Regiment moved by rail to Dombås to reinforce the Norwegians there. Two companies of the 8th Sherwood Foresters moved by rail farther south to Lillehammer. There, Brigadier General Morgan established 148th Brigade headquarters and linked up with part of the Norwegian 5th Infantry Regiment and one battalion of the Norwegian 4th Infantry Regiment preparing to defend the entrance to Gudbrandsdal from the Germans.

The British and Germans clash

Mauriceforce moved 146th Brigade south by road and on 18 April occupied the town of Steinkjer, a key position on the Trondheim Fjord where the rail line to Trondheim intersected the road to Trondheim. The British had linked up with some Norwegian battalions and were now only 70km from Trondheim. On 19 April, 4,000 French *chasseurs alpins* troops arrived in Namsos, but the small size of the docks there made it impossible to unload heavy equipment from the large transport ship and General de Wiart could not send the French forward. Still, 146th Brigade advanced cautiously beyond Steinkjer.

German air power had been constrained between 12 and 19 April by weather, the poor condition of Værnes airfield, and runway damage from the RAF attacks on Stavanger. But the Germans now had bombers and at least four Ju 87s operating from Værnes, while Stavanger had been repaired and was in full operation. The German counter-attack began on 20 April, when waves of German bombers from Stavanger levelled the town of Namsos. There were only a few casualties, but a great part of Mauriceforce's supplies and many vehicles were destroyed. On 21 April, a task force of 2,500 troops advanced on the British/Norwegian positions south of Steinkjer. The Germans were supported by gunfire from destroyers and S-boats on Trondheim Fjord as well as artillery. The Kriegsmarine vessels landed German troops on the flank of the Allied line. The Germans were well supported by bombers and the Ju 87s stationed nearby in Trondheim. Steinkjer, headquarters of 146th Brigade, was given the same treatment as Namsos the day before and reduced to ruins. Holding Steinkjer was impossible in the face of superior German firepower, and on 23 April General de Wiart informed the army headquarters in London that he had no alternative but to withdraw Mauriceforce back to Namsos.

In central Norway Gruppe Pellengahr attacked the British and Norwegians dug in at Lillehammer on the afternoon of 21 April. His attack was preceded by a heavy artillery barrage, and air strikes from KG 4. General Morgan's small British force, with no artillery and limited ammunition, were forced to retreat. The next day, the Germans continued the attack with air and artillery support as well as tanks and outflanked the British defence lines. On 23 April, 148th Brigade, reinforced by two more companies of the Leicestershire Regiment, attempted to build a defence line in the excellent defensive ground in the Tretten Gorge where they hoped to hold the German advance for two or three days until reinforcements and heavy weapons arrived from Åndalsnes. However, the next day Pellengahr's task force,

Namsos after the heavy German aerial bombardment of 20 April 1940. The town, containing most of the supplies of Mauriceforce, was completely levelled by the German attack. (Keystone-France/Gamma-Keystone via Getty Images)

heavily supported by air attacks, artillery and tanks, broke through the British/Norwegian defences, effectively destroying 148th Brigade, with 706 British officers and enlisted men dead, missing or captured.

Remnants of the brigade escaped north, but the commander General Morgan was captured, and 148th Brigade broken. The British 15th Brigade, drawn from the British Expeditionary Force in France, landed in Åndalsnes on 23 April but could not move south rapidly enough to reinforce the 148th Brigade. The 15th Brigade had only its infantry units and a single anti-tank company, as the transport ship bringing the brigade's artillery, vehicles and supplies had been sunk en route by a U-boat. The new British commander of Sickleforce was Major General Bernard Paget. With the 15th Brigade and parts of the Norwegian 2nd Division, he established a strong new defence line at Kvam, 55km south of Dombås. At Kvam, the 15th Brigade managed to hold the German advance for two days, and the anti-tank guns of the brigade destroyed three German tanks. Until this time, the Germans had faced no anti-tank guns, for the Norwegian Army in 1940 had none. The Germans slowly pushed the Allied defence line at Kvam back, with constant attacks by KG 4's He 111 bombers playing a major role in reducing the British defences.

To the east, the German task force under Colonel Fischer had steadily advanced through the Østerdal and was now in position to effect a linkup with German forces advancing south from Trondheim. They were also in position to send a column west to attack the key rail junction at Dombås which connected the road and rail lines from Åndalsnes to Trondheim. The loss of Dombås would mean the destruction of Sickleforce. The British/Norwegian force was now in an untenable position. The advance group of Colonel Fischer's battle group was in position to drive west and cut off British forces retreating through Dombås. Colonel Fischer's force linked up with German units advancing south from Trondheim on 29 April. Germans could bring a numerical and firepower superiority against Sickleforce.

On 28 April, the British War Cabinet ordered the evacuation of Sickleforce from Norway. Mauriceforce was also preparing to evacuate through Namsos. On 29 April, King Haakon and the Norwegian government embarked on British warships and were evacuated to Bodø in the far north of Norway. The 15th Brigade and remnants of the 148th Brigade retreated to Åndalsnes, and most were evacuated on 30 April. The next day, 1 May, Major General Ruge and his staff were evacuated to Tromsø in northern Norway. Sickleforce had lost 1,301 soldiers killed, missing or captured in its two-week campaign in central Norway. However, the Royal Navy was able to evacuate 5,084 troops without any losses. The remnants of the Norwegian 2nd Division that had fought alongside the British surrendered on 3 May, ending all Allied resistance in central Norway.

British air support finally arrives

The carriers *Ark Royal* and *Glorious* had only been recalled from the Mediterranean on 16 April and could not arrive off Norway for several days, so for more than a week the Allied expeditionary forces in central Norway operated without any air support. Both Allied forces were desperate for air support, and it finally arrived on 24 April in the form of 18 Gladiators from No. 263 Squadron RAF, ferried from HMS *Glorious*. With no airfields in the region, the RAF identified a frozen lake, Lesjaskogsvatnet, 80km southeast of Åndalsnes, as the best place to operate fighters. It was a desperate, improvised operation. The Gladiators landed on the frozen lake after snow had been cleared, but squadron ground crew lacked basic equipment. There were no hangars, and aircraft had to be parked in the open. With no refuelling truck, aircraft were fuelled using milk cans borrowed from farmers. There was no machine-gun belt loading machine, so the fighters' machine guns had to be loaded by hand.

On 25 April No. 263 Squadron managed to send up some sorties to support Sickleforce defending Kvam. But early-morning Luftwaffe reconnaissance spotted the improvised airfield and by afternoon it was under heavy attack. The Gladiators defended their base and shot down six German bombers, but by evening the lake had been heavily bombed and 15 Gladiators destroyed on the ground. The next day, the squadron was evacuated back to Åndalsnes, and the three remaining aircraft were burned by the crews.

HMS *Ark Royal* and HMS *Glorious* finally took position 190km off the Norwegian coast on 24 April. It was already too late to impact the ground campaign, as Mauriceforce and Sickleforce had both been defeated and were retreating to be evacuated. For the next week, the Swordfish bombers and Skua fighters attempted to provide some air cover for the British forces, now evacuating. Swordfish from No. 820 Squadron from the *Ark Royal* bombed Værnes from 6,000ft but caused only light damage. Skua fighters from the *Ark Royal* and *Glorious* flew patrols over Åndalsnes and Namsos, where waves of German bombers arrived whenever the weather was flyable, in an attempt to deter them.

Allied shipping was the primary target for the bombers operating mainly from Stavanger airfield. To minimize their vulnerability to German bombers, the Allies ran the port operations mostly at night. But small ports with minimal facilities could not support large forces with only night operations, so in daylight the Luftwaffe found plenty of ship targets in port or just off the coast.

During World War II the Royal Navy put more than 200 small trawlers – coastal vessels of 300–700 tons mostly commandeered from the civilian merchant fleet – into service as Royal Navy vessels. While too short-ranged to serve as ocean-going vessels, the converted trawlers were useful as coastal minesweepers and anti-submarine patrol boats. Because they could carry personnel and cargo and were small enough to operate in small Norwegian ports, dozens were committed to support the Allied forces in Norway as light cargo vessels. The Royal Navy trawlers and the coastal merchant vessels of the Norwegian merchant marine would suffer heavily in the campaign in central Norway and then at Narvik.

HMS *Ark Royal*'s Swordfish biplane bomber. *Ark Royal*, built in 1937, was the Royal Navy's most modern aircraft carrier. Unlike the other carriers used in the campaign, *Ark Royal* had been purpose-built as an aircraft carrier. It normally carried 50–60 aircraft. (Haynes Archive/ Popperfoto via Getty Images)

Starting with the bombing of Namsos on 20 April, Allied shipping became the target of constant air attacks on every day that the weather allowed for moderate visibility. Because it was difficult to manoeuvre in the narrow fjords, German level bombers, such as the He 111, normally not effective against moving ships on the open sea, found ships in confined waters to be an easier target. On 20 April German bombers struck not only the town of Namsos but sank the anti-submarine trawler HMS *Rutlandshire* off Namsos. Åndalsnes, as well as Namsos, became a prime target for the Luftwaffe. On 24 April, the anti-aircraft cruiser HMS *Curacoa* was badly damaged by German bombers at Åndalsnes and had to return to Scapa Flow. The next day, three Royal Navy trawlers were sunk off Åndalsnes. Bad weather prevented Luftwaffe attacks for three days, but when the weather cleared on 29 April, three more Royal Navy trawlers were sunk. As the evacuation of Mauriceforce proceeded on 30 April, the sloop HMS *Bittern* was sunk at Namsos, and the trawler HMS *Warwickshire* was sunk off Trondheim. On 1 May the Luftwaffe sank another Royal Navy trawler at Namsos, and an anti-submarine trawler, HMS *Aston Villa* was badly damaged and was scuttled in the last stage of the Mauriceforce evacuation on 3 May.

The worst losses during the Allied evacuation from Åndalsnes and Namsos came during its last days. With Værnes airfield now rebuilt and able to base a large number of aircraft, the Ju 87s from StG 1, the Luftwaffe's most deadly ship-killers, could be based there and released against the evacuation convoys. The Ju 87 squadrons had developed an effective tactic of attacking ships at sea with pairs of Ju 87s. A Stuka would position to the left and right of a fast-moving ship, normally the toughest target to hit, and if the ship manoeuvred sharply to the left or right, one of the Stukas would be in position to bomb.

While the final evacuation at Åndalsnes was effected with no losses, the worst of the Allied losses came at the very end of the Namsos evacuation. On 2 May, the destroyer HMS *Afridi* escorting the last large evacuation convoy from Namsos was targeted by the Ju 87s and sunk. The large French destroyer *Bisson*, which stopped to pick up survivors from the *Afridi*, was also struck by Ju 87s and sank with large loss of life. On 3 May, the final day of the Namsos

Norwegian coastal town of Åndalsnes, burning after German air attack. Åndalsnes, as well as nearby Molde, suffered from repeated German bomber attacks from 20 to 30 April. (© Imperial War Museums, MH 31352)

evacuation, the trawler HMS *Gaul* was sunk by German bombers.

From 24 April until 2 May the Skua squadrons of the *Glorious* and *Ark Royal* flew cover for the fleet off Norway and tried to protect the ships carrying away Allied forces at Namsos and Åndalsnes. There were some successes. On 26 and 27 April, He 111s from KG 26 attacked the British cruiser HMS *Flamingo*, but Skuas managed to shoot down three of the He 111s and break up the attack. The British carriers were found and attacked by Luftwaffe bombers, and these were prime targets because Reichsmarschall Hermann

Åndalsnes burning after Luftwaffe air strike April 1940. (Author's collection)

Göring publicly promised a reward of 100,000 Reichsmarks to any pilot who sank a carrier. Both carriers came under attack and experienced some near misses, but the Skua fighters efficiently broke up the bomber raids. Skuas from HMS *Ark Royal* also flew fighter cover over Åndalsnes and shot down a He 111 from KG 4 on 26 April. In all, Fleet Air Arm fighters from HMS *Glorious* and HMS *Ark Royal* shot down 20 German aircraft during the last week of April, while losing 15 of their own number – several to operational accidents.

The British naval, air and ground campaign in central Norway had been a valiant, but terribly mismanaged, effort. It was doomed to failure by poor planning, poor intelligence and poor command and control. One of the signal British mistakes was the failure to develop effective liaison with the Norwegian forces. The British appointed a military attaché to the Norwegian government, but never provided a liaison team with communications to coordinate efforts with General Ruge. The British commanders doubted the Norwegian Army's fighting ability and failed to include the Norwegian commanders fighting alongside in operational planning. On 15 April, at the start of the Allied intervention, General Ruge sent the British commanders a list of airfield sites in central Norway that could be used, or if not, neutralized, by the British. Like most of General Ruge's advice, it was ignored. The Norwegians were not told of the Allied evacuation until the last minute, and most Norwegian forces in central Norway were left behind to surrender.

HMS *Glorious*, converted into an aircraft carrier from a World War I battlecruiser, carried up to 48 aircraft. In late April, the Sea Gladiators flew cover for *Glorious* and *Ark Royal* in operations off the central Norway coast. Swordfish bombers from *Glorious* attacked land targets at Trondheim. (US Navy)

Through the campaign in central Norway the Luftwaffe provided the Germans with a decisive advantage. Although the RAF carried out reconnaissance flights of German airfields and ports, it was spotty and there was no attempt to conduct air reconnaissance behind the German Army lines. In contrast, the German reconnaissance effort was extensive and covered all of southern and central Norway and the North Sea. Both long-range reconnaissance aircraft and the short-range Hs 126s of the army cooperation squadron overflew the British and Norwegian rear areas, observing road and rail movement and the layout of defence lines. Luftwaffe reconnaissance was pervasive enough to find

the improvised RAF airfield at Lesjaskogsvatnet as soon as it was established. With good intelligence, supported by an excellent communications and liaison system between army and Luftwaffe, the German bombers had accurate target information. Air attacks on Allied front-line units were accurate and devastating. Interdiction of road movement in the Allied rear restricted Allied movements. Finally, in the assessments of the British commanders, the powerful attacks on the two Allied ports destroyed so many vehicles and supplies that minimal logistics for the troops could not be assured. It is likely that the German Army would have defeated the Allies without air power. But it was German air power, expertly wielded, that enabled the Germans to advance quickly through central Norway. The rapidity of the German advance, the flexibility to quickly respond to Allied actions, and the ability to synchronize Luftwaffe and army operations ended a campaign that, in the previous world war, would have taken months.

Reorganizing the Luftwaffe for the fight in the north

With Værnes airfield rebuilt and fully operational, and following the British abandonment of central Norway, the Germans could now reinforce and supply their forces in Trondheim directly by rail from Oslo. Troops and supplies could be brought up immediately to begin a land advance to relieve Narvik. Narvik was now within range of German bombers since the Ju 52 transports, which had not had the range to reach Narvik, could now stage through Værnes and refuel. Consequently, personnel and supplies could now be air-dropped much more easily than before. On 21 April Hitler released 2. Gebirgs-Division, an elite unit like 3. Gebirgs-Division, to reinforce Gruppe XXI. For an advance into Norway's far north, it was the ideal unit.

With the British withdrawn from central Norway and Trondheim secured, the Luftwaffe's mission was to patrol the North Sea and defend the harbours and airfields of southern and central Norway, and to support a land and air offensive against the Allied forces besieging Narvik. General Milch again reorganized Luftflotte 5. In late April, Milch had received some reinforcements with the addition of the pathfinder group from Lehrgeschwader 1 (LG 1) as well as a squadron of the Fw 200 Condors. The Condors were modified four-engine, long-range passenger aircraft that had been the pride of Lufthansa's international travel in the late 1930s. Now, heavily armed and able to carry large bombloads, the Condors proved to be good platforms for long-range anti-shipping strikes. To reinforce the transport force, X Fliegerkorps also received the five prototype Blohm & Voss BV 138 and 139a flying boats and five Dornier Do 26 flying boats.

However, in early May Milch had to send most of his bombers and transports back to support the German spring offensive in the West. Luftflotte 5 was left with three medium bomber groups, and squadrons from LG 1 and some FW 200 Condors, over 100 bombers. The 40 Stukas of StG 1 remained as well as the Bf 110 fighters of ZG 76. It was enough for the final campaign in Norway.

Milch appointed X Fliegerkorps Chief of Staff Lieutenant Colonel Martin Harlinghausen as Fliegerführer at Stavanger and reorganized that task force to consist of 80 aircraft, mostly fighters and reconnaissance aircraft. Colonel Rudolf Fuchs, Fliegerführer at Stavanger in April, took command as Fliegerführer of Trondheim, which had been reorganized into a task force. Fuchs' force had approximately 190 aircraft, including most of the bombers of X Fliegerkorps. Two groups of KG 26, equipped with He 111s, went to Trondheim where they became the main bomber force against the Allies at Narvik. Two squadrons of bombers as well as patrol aircraft and fighters were stationed in Aalborg, which served to secure the southern flank of the North Sea.

The Fw 200 Condor was a late 1930s four-engine civilian airliner designed to carry passengers or cargo for long distances. The Fw 200 was modified by the Luftwaffe as a maritime bomber. With a range of 1,600km, a speed of 240mph and able to carry up to 5,400kg of bombs, it was a very formidable anti-shipping aircraft. The Luftwaffe had only a few Fw 200s and six were committed to Norway, at first used as transports, but later used to bomb Allied shipping in the waters off Harstad. (Author's collection)

Luftwaffe General Hans-Jürgen Stumpff (right), talking to two of his staff officers. General Stumpff commanded Luftflotte 5 during the last stages of the Norway campaign from 10 May through the fall of Narvik. Stumpff, a former Luftwaffe chief of staff, proved a very capable field commander, reorganizing the Luftwaffe forces in Norway to support the ground offensive from Trondheim to Bodø, while also putting the British forces at Harstad under heavy pressure. (Mondadori via Getty Images)

With central Norway occupied, the Germans could now transport troops and supplies directly by rail from Oslo to Trondheim. However, it took several days after the Allied withdrawal to prepare Trondheim for the offensive to the north as supply problems persisted. Much of the aviation fuel that had been shipped to Trondheim by U-boats had become contaminated by water on the voyage and was unusable. However, with central Norway secure in mid-May and the British submarine operations reduced due to their losses and more effective German anti-submarine patrols, the Germans could resume sea transport. A ship convoy arrived in Trondheim in mid-May carrying aviation fuel and ample munitions, so Fliegerführer Trondheim now had ample logistics.

With the start of the spring offensive in the West, Milch was needed more in Berlin than in Norway. Command of Luftflotte 5 was turned over to General Hans-Jürgen Stumpff. Stumpff moved easily into the job as he came from command of Luftflotte 1. Although operating with fewer than half the aircraft that had been available to X Fliegerkorps on 9 April, his remaining forces were still more than adequate for the final acts of the campaign.

The battle for Narvik: April–June

The Allied land campaign to retake Narvik from the Germans began with the landing of the British 24th Brigade at Harstad, a small port town at the mouth of the Ofotfjord, some 55km from Narvik, on 14 April. At Harstad British ground forces commander Major General Pierse Mackesy met with Major General Carl Fleischer, commander of the Norwegian 6th Division. The 6th Division was the only division of the Norwegian Army fully mobilized on 9 April,

Some of the German I. Battalion/1. Fallschirmjäger-Regiment soldiers dropping near Narvik to reinforce the garrison in the second half of May 1940. The Luftwaffe flew in 600 reinforcements to support General Dietl's force of mountain troops and improvised naval battalions. (ullstein bild via Getty Images)

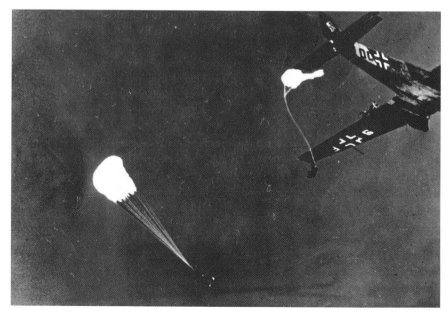

set to guard the Norwegian-Soviet border in the far north of Norway in case of spillover from the Soviet-Finnish War. Fleischer moved about half his division of more than 8,000 men, equipped for winter combat, south towards Harstad to set up a defensive line in the mostly mountainous terrain north of Narvik. With the arrival of the 24th Brigade, the combined British-Norwegian ground forces already greatly outnumbered Generalleutnant Dietl's approximately 4,400 men. Dietl's only fully trained army unit was 139. Gebirgs-Regiment. The rest were naval personnel armed and equipped with captured Norwegian weapons, as well as some of the guns salvaged off the four German destroyers beached in Rombaksfjord after the second naval battle for Narvik.

Lieutenant General Claude Auchinleck, appointed as commander of Allied ground troops at Narvik in May 1940. Auchinleck showed sound leadership and was a highly competent ground commander. However, his arrival came far too late to save the situation in northern Norway. (Keystone-France/Gamma-Rapho via Getty Images)

Despite having the advantage in forces and having the firepower of the Royal Navy to support him, General Mackesy faced a host of problems. The docks of Harstad could not handle a heavy volume of logistics traffic, and the equipment and weapons that arrived slowly were often missing components. Thousands of tons of supplies lay about the harbour in disorder. Artillery and anti-aircraft guns would not arrive until the end of the month. So, the British commander proceeded to set up a proper base for a large force before advancing on the Germans.

Generalleutnant Dietl deployed his one mountain infantry regiment in a long and thinly held line in the mountains and plateaux 25km north of Narvik, while basing his improvised naval infantry battalions at likely Allied landing points near the town of Narvik and along Narvik's waterfront. While awaiting Allied reinforcements, the Norwegian 6th Division began an offensive against the German northern flank on 23 April, pushing the German defence lines back in places. Under extreme weather conditions, including blizzards, the Norwegians gained key ground at Gratangsboten but soon lost it to a German counter-attack. This, and the weather, led to a stalemate. The Allied situation improved when the 27e Demi-Brigade de Chasseurs Alpins arrived at Harstad on 28 April. Brigadier General Antoine Béthouart moved his brigade, supported by a French artillery regiment, up to join the Norwegians on 4 May. The Germans held good defensive ground, but the Allied superiority in men and firepower was bound to win. The Germans were pushed back on 10 May to a new defence line close to Narvik. On 6 May more reinforcements arrived when the 13e Demi-Brigade of the French Foreign Legion arrived at Harstad, followed by the Polish Podhale (Rifles) Brigade on 9 May. The Allied land forces now held a 5:1 manpower superiority over the Germans.

As the Allied force was built up at Harstad, the Allied High Command replaced the cautious General Mackesy with Lt General Claude Auchinleck, who arrived on 13 May with a corps headquarters. Auchinleck quickly approved plans for amphibious landings along the Ofotfjord north and south of Narvik, catching the Germans in a pincer movement that would be supported by heavy Allied naval gunfire.

The Luftwaffe's desperate supply efforts at Narvik

With the shock of the Royal Navy's destruction of all the German destroyers at Narvik on 10 and 13 April, as well as the loss of their supply ships, Hitler panicked about the fate of the German forces at Narvik, cut off and surrounded by Allied forces. OKW responded to

Airdrop of supplies at Narvik, 1940. Some heavy weapons and ammunition were airdropped to resupply General Dietl's force in May 1940. (Author's collection)

Hitler's fears by organizing relief operations by air for Generalleutnant Dietl's stranded forces. The OKW negotiated with Sweden to allow the transit of troops and equipment through their border, which lay only a few kilometres east of Narvik. The Swedes, guarding their neutrality, denied the request to transport troops and equipment, but did allow transit of non-military supplies by rail to Dietl's force. Trainloads of food and medical supplies allowed through Sweden assured the Germans of months of rations and medical supplies for a large force. Approximately 200 German military personnel were slipped in with the Swedish shipments, posing as medical personnel. However, the Swedes were adamant that no arms, ammunition, or regular troops would be allowed through Sweden. Yet it was heavy weapons, ammunition and soldiers that Dietl desperately needed.

Narvik lay 1,000km in direct flight from Oslo, well beyond the range of the Ju 52 transports, which compromised more than 80 per cent of all the Luftwaffe's transport capability. The Luftwaffe had at its disposal only a handful of large cargo aircraft with the range to fly to Narvik and drop supplies. At the start of the war, the Luftwaffe requisitioned two Junkers Ju 90 transport planes in the hands of Lufthansa. The Ju 90 was an outgrowth of the four-engine bomber programme proposed in the mid-1930s. Rejected as a bomber, the Ju 90 prototypes were rebuilt as long-range heavy cargo and passenger aircraft. These four-engine aeroplanes could carry 5 tons of cargo – and for shorter hauls, as much as 10. The two available Ju 90 transports were allocated to X Fliegerkorps transport wings. In addition, another large transport aircraft, a Junkers G 38, had been commandeered by the Luftwaffe. The G 38 first flew in 1929; at the time, it was the largest cargo aircraft in the world. Slow but rugged, it had been built for long-range passenger travel and it could carry several tons of cargo to Narvik.

At the outbreak of the war, the Focke-Wulf Fw 200 Condor, a four-engine aircraft built as a long-distance passenger plane, was the pride of the national airline. X Fliegerkorps had four Fw 200s, former civilian aircraft modified for military use. The Luftwaffe was also creating squadrons of Fw 200s to carry bombs, heavy machine guns and cannon, and employ them as long-range anti-shipping aircraft as they could fly long distances and patrol far beyond the range of any Allied fighter planes. The Luftwaffe's coastal patrol units were equipped with some flying boats, including the Dornier Do 18, which had two engines mounted tandem and was used for naval reconnaissance. More than 20 Do 18s were assigned to *Weserübung*. These aircraft, able to land on Norwegian coastal waters, played an important role transporting troops and supplies during the campaign, but the Do 18 did not have the range to carry cargo to Narvik. Indeed, to provide additional transport capability for the campaign, the Luftwaffe scrounged up a variety of prototype flying boats that could carry cargo. Two prototypes of the Do 24 flying boat, designed in Germany but built under licence in Holland, were assigned to Küstenfliegergruppe 108, and these three-engine aircraft had considerable range. The Luftwaffe also had five large Dornier Do 26 flying boats assigned to the 1st Squadron of Küstenfliegergruppe 506, and these aircraft could transport passengers and supplies. The Blohm & Voss BV 138 three-engine flying boats were so new they had not yet been fully tested for service, but they could carry 3 tons of cargo and had a range of 1,220km. The first two prototypes were assigned to Küstenfliegergruppe 108, part of the transport forces of *Weserübung*. However, given the tactical situation, most of the long-range flying boats were used to fly troops and supplies to Bergen and Trondheim.

OKW's first plan to get immediate support to Generalleutnant Dietl's troops at Narvik was to load 13 Ju 52 transports from KGr zbV 102 to meet Dietl's desperate need for artillery. A battery of lightweight 75mm Skoda mountain guns and 65 artillerymen from 112. Gebirgsartillerie Regiment, with as much ammunition as could be carried, was loaded in aircraft in Germany and refuelled at Oslo. Narvik had no airfield so they flew to Lake Hartvig, a frozen lake a few kilometres from Narvik that Dietl identified as the best available landing ground. However, the Ju 52

Flight of Stukas from StG 1 over Norway. The Ju 87R dive bomber of StG 1 had extra fuel tanks for extended range. It carried 500kg bombs and was the Luftwaffe's most accurate bomber in 1940 and highly effective in the campaign in providing close air support and in the anti-shipping role. (Author's collection)

lacked the range to fly to Narvik and return. So, a mission was planned for the following day to send three Ju 52s loaded with fuel to allow the transport squadron to return.

The transports made it to Narvik on 13 April and delivered the guns and men, but the ice at Lake Hartvig had been weakened by a thaw that day. The wheels of eight transports cracked the ice, then froze into the lake surface when the temperature turned cold again. With no heavy equipment, the Germans had no means to pull the planes free. The refuelling planes could not come due to bad weather, so the squadron commander fuelled two of the stranded Ju 52s for a return flight by siphoning off the remaining fuel in the other aircraft. The return flight went wrong when one pilot aborted the takeoff due to heavy snow on the lake, and the lone aircraft that got aloft strayed across the border into Sweden, where it was forced to land and the aircraft and crew interned by the Swedish military. The Ju 52 squadron was now frozen solidly into Lake Hartvig's surface, providing target practice for the Norwegian Army air detachment of old Fokker CV biplanes operating out of nearby Bardufoss airfield. Several of the Ju 52s were bombed and shot to pieces before the remaining aircraft sank into the lake during the late spring thaws.

With this debacle, the only way to send aid to Narvik was to airdrop supplies from the few long-range transports available: the Fw 200s, the Ju 90s and the G 38. To save on the cost of parachutes, some of the first shipments of anti-tank guns and ammunition were wrapped and dropped in the snow without a parachute. Guns and most supplies dropped this way were wrecked. Only in early May, after Trondheim was secure, could Narvik be supplied and reinforced by flying boats that could land on Rombaksfjord next to the city. But by then, the strong Allied forces in Harstad, with their anti-aircraft batteries and the anti-aircraft guns of the Royal Navy, made flying to Narvik a dangerous proposition.

A further scheme to reinforce Narvik was a programme to train soldiers of 3. Gebirgs-Division in a brief paratroop course and then airdrop them at Narvik. Germany's trained paratroopers of the Luftwaffe's 7. Fallschirmjäger-Division were already committed to the attack on the Netherlands on 10 May; even after the Netherlands fell, the paratroop units would need time to refit and transport the paratroopers to Norway. Late May was the earliest period when paratroopers could be available, and even then no mass drops could be made, as most of Germany's transport forces were committed to support the armies and air fleets fighting in France.

It was six weeks after Generalleutnant Dietl had conquered Narvik that the first paratroop reinforcements were dropped. Staging through Trondheim, a detachment of hastily assembled 137. Gebirgs-Jägerregiment soldiers were successfully parachuted into the Narvik pocket on 23 May. Over the next two days, another 150 mountain troops were dropped in small detachments. The 1st Battalion of 1. Fallschirmjäger-Regiment that had fought in

Paratroop drop at Narvik, May 1940. General Dietl's isolated force at Narvik was reinforced by more than 600 troops, most of them mountain troops given a hasty parachute course. (Author's collection)

Holland began to arrive on 26 May. Between 23 May and 2 June, 600 mountain troops and paratroopers had been dropped to support Dietl. This programme of aerial reinforcement and supply provided some relief to Generalleutnant Dietl's embattled garrison and brought the size of his force to over 5,000 men. However, being outnumbered more than 5:1 by the Allied forces and vastly outnumbered in terms of firepower, with Royal Navy battleships, cruisers and destroyers arrayed against him, the situation for the Germans at Narvik looked hopeless.

The German land offensive north to Bodø

Hitler ordered 2. Gebirgs-Division to reinforce Gruppe XXI in Norway on 21 April and it was quickly shipped to Trondheim. 2. Gebirgs-Division, like the 3rd, was a superbly trained elite formation, equipped to operate in Norway's Arctic conditions. From Trondheim units of 2. Gebirgs-Division proceeded 200km north to the town of Grong, the terminus of a rail line running from Trondheim. The Germans established a logistics base at Grong and on 5 May began a land advance north towards the town of Bodø, 250km away. Bodø was only 200km from Harstad. If the Germans could take it and establish an airbase within easy range for the Stukas to attack Allied shipping, then Narvik would be untenable.

Commanded by Lieutenant General Valentin von Feuerstein, 2. Gebirgs-Division was organized around seven mountain infantry battalions, two artillery battalions, and included bicycle troops, a motorized machine-gun unit and engineers. Von Feuerstein's force would grow to more than 6,000 and could count on aerial resupply if the roads running north from Grong became impassable. Facing the German offensive were two under-strength Norwegian battalions. General Mackesy recognized this threat and sent forces south to block the Germans. Mackesy's force now included four independent companies, forerunners of the commandos, sent to Bodø. Mosjøen, a town 174km south of Bodø, was selected to be the main point of defence; two independent companies and two light anti-aircraft guns were dispatched there to link up with the Norwegian battalions.

Without waiting for the entire 2. Gebirgs-Division to arrive, von Feuerstein moved with three battalions, supported by two artillery batteries, engineers and a motorized machine-gun unit, and began the advance northward on 5 May. At this time, the primary focus of Fliegerführer Trondheim was supporting the ground advance to Bodø, although some long-range missions were flown against the Allied naval forces at Harstad.

The two British independent companies arrived at Mosjøen on the night of 8–9 May as the Germans were approaching the town. On 10 May, after some skirmishing, the superior German forces overran Mosjøen, and the Norwegian and British units retreated north on 11 May to set up defences at Mo i Rana. General Mackesy, alarmed by the rapid advance of von Feuerstein's force, ordered the entire 24th Brigade south to protect Bodø on 9 May. The British reinforcements suffered from a series of mishaps. On 14 May, the British commander of the force sent to defend the Bodø area was taken out of action when the destroyer he was sailing on, HMS *Somali*, was bombed by the Luftwaffe. Severely damaged, it was forced to divert to Scapa Flow along with the force commander. On the same day, the Polish troopship *Chrobry*, carrying the 24th Brigade headquarters and a battalion of the Irish Guards, was bombed and sunk en route to Bodø. Many officers of the Irish Guards battalion were killed, including the commander. Though 700 troops were rescued from the *Chrobry*, the battalion had lost all its equipment and was taken out of the battle. The next attempt to reinforce Bodø came on 17 May, when the British cruiser HMS *Effingham*, carrying the 2nd

Battery of heavy 3.7in British anti-aircraft guns defending Harstad, May 1940. (© Imperial War Museums, IWM HU 104678)

Battalion, 24th South Wales Borderers, ran aground at high speed near Bodø. All the troops were taken off the ship, but the equipment was lost – and another battalion withdrawn from the battle. Only a single battalion of 24th Brigade, 1st Scots Guards, made it safely to Bodø, along with a few guns.

In the meantime, the Germans continued their steady advance, aided by Blohm & Voss BV 138 and Do 24 flying boats landing on small coastal fjords to bring in supplies. Ju 52 transports dropped supplies to the lead elements of 2. Gebirgs-Division, now increased to 6,000 men. On 10 May advancing Germans located a small Norwegian airfield at Hattfjelldal 30km southeast of Mosjøen that was suitable to base the Ju 87s. While Bodø and Narvik were out of range of the Stukas, the airfield at Hattfjelldal brought Bodø and Harstad into range of the Luftwaffe's most effective anti-ship bombers.

The British brought three companies of 1st Battalion Scots Guards to Mo i Rana and established defence lines at Stein, to the south. The Germans attacked on 17 May and dropped a platoon of paratroops from four Ju 52s to seize a position on the British right flank, while the German main force attacked on the left flank. In danger of being cut off, The British retreated north the next day. Because two battalions of reinforcements had failed to reach Bodø, the Allies could field only 4,500 troops to man a new defence line south of Bodø while von Feuerstein's force numbered more than 6,000 and had artillery and ample air support. Moreover, there was little cover in the coastal terrain and German air superiority allowed them to conduct reconnaissance and bombing with little interference.

On 20 May the Allies continued their retreat, hoping to set up a defence near Bodø. With the defeat of the British and French armies in northern France and the evacuation at Dunkirk looming, the Allied Supreme War Council decided on 24 May to end the Norway expedition and evacuate the country. The Allied forces in Norway could take Narvik to destroy the port facilities to prevent the shipment of Swedish iron ore, but they must then fully evacuate the country. On 25 May, General Auchinleck ordered Allied forces to evacuate Bodø. In a last-minute effort to provide air support for the British forces at Bodø and help protect the evacuation, three Gladiators from RAF No. 263 Squadron arrived at a small landing field near the port. One Gladiator was quickly taken out of action when it crashed because of the mud on the scarcely usable airstrip. But on the 26th, the two remaining Gladiators shot down four German aircraft, including two Ju 52 transports carrying paratroopers to Narvik and a Ju 87 bombing the town. Escorting German Bf 110s shot down the two Gladiators, and on 27 May the Stukas returned and carried out a massive attack on Bodø, levelling more than half of the town and destroying most of the British supplies. The last ship evacuated

The battle of Narvik

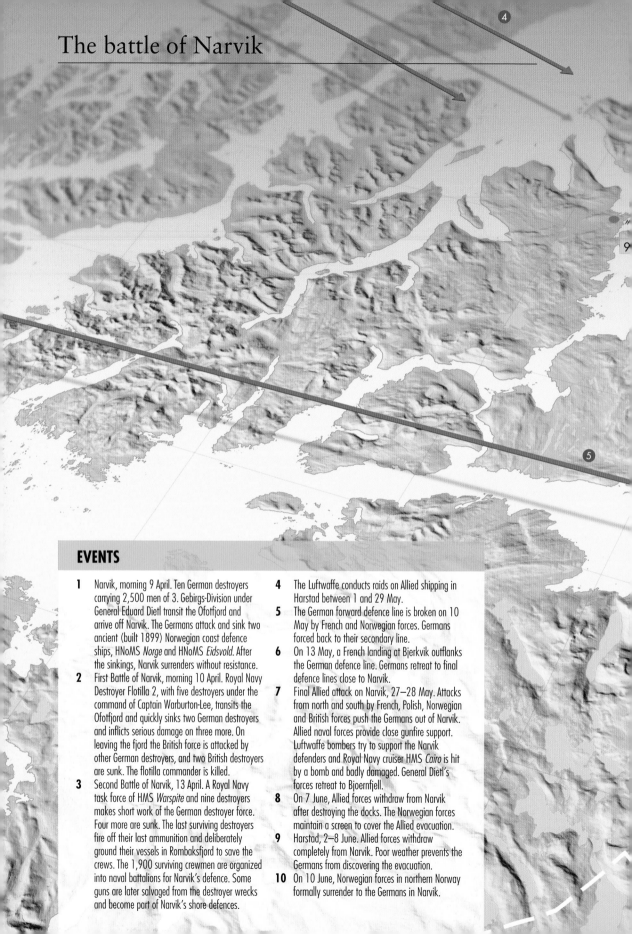

EVENTS

1 Narvik, morning 9 April. Ten German destroyers carrying 2,500 men of 3. Gebirgs-Division under General Eduard Dietl transit the Ofotfjord and arrive off Narvik. The Germans attack and sink two ancient (built 1899) Norwegian coast defence ships, HNoMS *Norge* and HNoMS *Eidsvold*. After the sinkings, Narvik surrenders without resistance.

2 First Battle of Narvik, morning 10 April. Royal Navy Destroyer Flotilla 2, with five destroyers under the command of Captain Warburton-Lee, transits the Ofotfjord and quickly sinks two German destroyers and inflicts serious damage on three more. On leaving the fjord the British force is attacked by other German destroyers, and two British destroyers are sunk. The flotilla commander is killed.

3 Second Battle of Narvik, 13 April. A Royal Navy task force of HMS *Warspite* and nine destroyers makes short work of the German destroyer force. Four more are sunk. The last surviving destroyers fire off their last ammunition and deliberately ground their vessels in Rombaksfjord to save the crews. The 1,900 surviving crewmen are organized into naval battalions for Narvik's defence. Some guns are later salvaged from the destroyer wrecks and become part of Narvik's shore defences.

4 The Luftwaffe conducts raids on Allied shipping in Harstad between 1 and 29 May.

5 The German forward defence line is broken on 10 May by French and Norwegian forces. Germans forced back to their secondary line.

6 On 13 May, a French landing at Bjerkvik outflanks the German defence line. Germans retreat to final defence lines close to Narvik.

7 Final Allied attack on Narvik, 27–28 May. Attacks from north and south by French, Polish, Norwegian and British forces push the Germans out of Narvik. Allied naval forces provide close gunfire support. Luftwaffe bombers try to support the Narvik defenders and Royal Navy cruiser HMS *Cairo* is hit by a bomb and badly damaged. General Dietl's forces retreat to Bjoernfjell.

8 On 7 June, Allied forces withdraw from Narvik after destroying the docks. The Norwegian forces maintain a screen to cover the Allied evacuation.

9 Harstad, 2–8 June. Allied forces withdraw completely from Narvik. Poor weather prevents the Germans from discovering the evacuation.

10 On 10 June, Norwegian forces in northern Norway formally surrender to the Germans in Narvik.

Air operations

1. Lake Hartvig. A frozen lake approximately 13km from Narvik. On 13 April, 13 Ju 52 transports land a mountain battery of 75mm guns and their crews as reinforcements for General Dietl. Due to a sudden thaw, most aircraft are frozen in the ice and cannot take off. Only one transport manages a takeoff, and gets lost and lands in Sweden, where it is interned.
2. Rombaksfjord. A fjord bordering the north side of Narvik. From 3–27 May, German flying boats land here and bring personnel and supplies to General Dietl's force.
3. Bjoernfjell. Rail terminus by the Swedish border. The Germans make this their main supply base. During the campaign German transports drop supplies here. From 23 May to 2 June 600 paratroops are dropped here to reinforce the German Narvik garrison. For the final defence of Narvik General Dietl will have over 5,000 troops, facing more than five times as many Allied troops.

Air operations

4. Luftwaffe raids on Allied shipping in Narvik area, 1–29 May. Luftwaffe bombers inflict significant losses to Allied shipping once Trondheim's Værnes Airfield is rebuilt. An air task force of 150 bombers, Stukas and long-range Bf 110 fighters are deployed to Trondheim in early May.
5. Weather on 28–29 May allows the Germans to make heavy air attacks against the Allied fleet, which has now moved forward to support the 27–28 May attack on Narvik. Ju 88 and He 111 bombers from KG 30, KG 26 and KGr 100, supported by Bf 110 fighters, make several large (25-plus aircraft) attacks on the Allied fleet and ground forces, usually flying bomb runs at 6,000–8,000ft.
6. Route of RAF fighters to patrol over Narvik. Fighters climb slowly from Bardufoss to Narvik, where they then circle at 15,000ft. A detachment of Norwegian Fokker CV two-seat biplanes is stationed here and fly support missions for the Norwegian 6th Division. On 21 May, No. 263 Squadron RAF with 18 Gladiators arrives. On 26 May, No. 46 Squadron RAF with Mark I Hurricanes arrives. Both squadrons evacuated to HMS Glorious on 7 June. The two RAF fighter squadrons will shoot down more than 30 Luftwaffe aircraft between 21 May and 7 June.

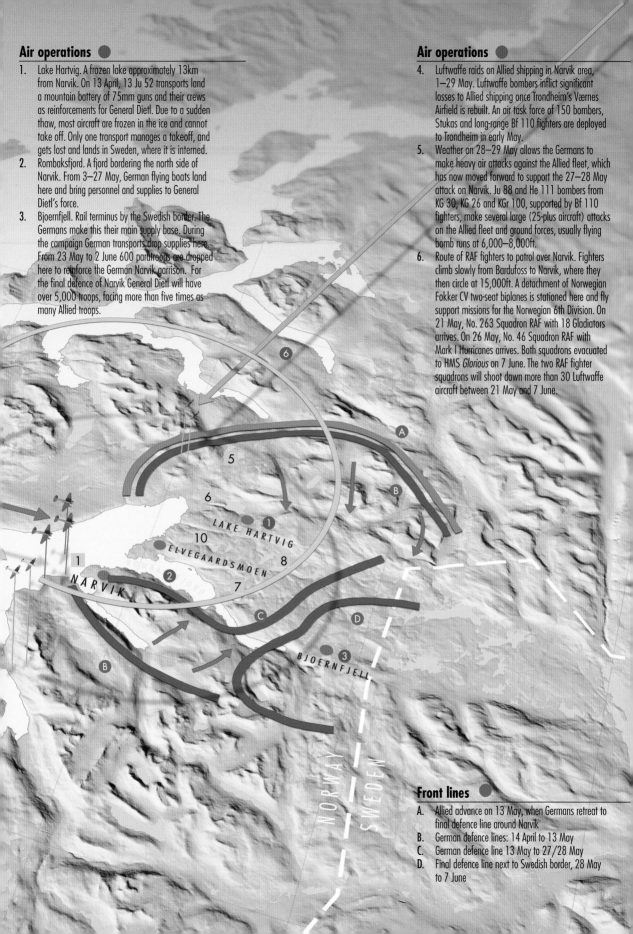

Front lines

A. Allied advance on 13 May, when Germans retreat to final defence line around Narvik
B. German defence lines: 14 April to 13 May
C. German defence line 13 May to 27/28 May
D. Final defence line next to Swedish border, 28 May to 7 June

General Nikolaus von Falkenhorst (1885–1968), German commander of Gruppe XXI in Norway. Von Falkenhorst had been a staff officer and operations officer for two major amphibious operations in World War I (both highly successful), so was one of the few senior commanders in 1940 who understood the detailed planning necessary for landing operations. Von Falkenhorst had proved himself a very capable corps commander in the Polish campaign. He again proved himself a very competent commander in Norway. (Klaus Niermann/ullstein bild via Getty Images)

from Bodø on 1 June carrying the British units as well as one Norwegian battalion. With the town now in German hands, and Harstad now within range of Ju 87s, the Allied situation at Narvik became even more untenable. Yet the Germans did not know that the Allies had decided to evacuate and in Narvik a nervous Generalleutnant Dietl readied his final defence lines against the expected Allied attack.

The Luftwaffe air offensive against Harstad

After the withdrawal of the Allied forces from central Norway, Luftflotte 5 intensified its reconnaissance and bomber patrols in the Narvik region. It was a target-rich environment for the Germans, with the growing Allied force at Harstad requiring many cargo ships and transports. The greater part of the large Norwegian merchant marine was now in the service of the Allies and shipping troops and supplies from Britain to Narvik. Small Norwegian coastal vessels ran troops and supplies from Harstad to the Allied base at Bodø. A considerable naval force was concentrated near Narvik that included French and Polish ships as well as Royal Navy battleships and cruisers. The Allies had a lot of shipping and not enough anti-aircraft guns to provide adequate protection.

The German air offensive against Narvik began on 1 May when a Norwegian cargo ship was sunk off Narvik. On 4 May, the Polish destroyer *Grom* was sunk, and on 5 May a British cargo vessel was sunk near Søreisa, near Harstad. On 7 May a Norwegian coastal vessel was bombed and sunk near Narvik. A few days of bad weather intervened, but at mid-month Luftflotte 5, now reorganized and based largely at Trondheim's Værnes airfield, was ready to mount an increasing number of attacks. As the days lengthened and there was little night in the northern latitudes, the Germans could attack at almost any hour if the weather were clear. On 14 May, the large Polish liner *Chrobry* was sunk while carrying troops to Bodø. Two days later Luftwaffe bombers spotted the battleship HMS *Resolution*, which had been at Harstad since late April, and managed to hit it with a 500kg bomb, causing damage and 29 casualties. On 19 May *Resolution* was withdrawn to Britain. From 19 to 24 May the Luftwaffe sank seven ships at Harstad, or in the approaches to Narvik. Most were smaller cargo vessels, one was a naval supply ship, and one a Royal Navy trawler.

As the Allies were in position to make a final attack to seize Narvik, a major effort was made by Fliegerführer Trondheim to provide air support by attacking the Allied fleet, but also to attack the Allied ground troops. General von Falkenhorst demanded air strikes on the Allied front lines at Narvik, and Colonel Fuchs strongly resisted diverting any effort away from the Allied ships. Fuchs sensibly pointed out that ground targets were hard to find and bomb with any effect and that attacks on shipping would damage the Allies far more. However, Luftflotte commander General Stumpff agreed to von Falkenhorst's requests and some bombers were diverted to ground targets. As Colonel Fuchs had predicted, not much damage was done, but seeing their bombers overhead provided Generalleutnant Dietl's beleaguered forces with a morale boost.

On 26 May, waves of German bombers, escorted by Bf 110s, attacked the Harstad anchorage. The Royal Navy cruiser HMS *Curlew* was hit and sunk by a Ju 88. That day also saw the Luftwaffe sink a Royal Navy patrol ship, HMS *Loch Shin*, and a naval tanker, the *Oleander*. When the final Allied ground attack on Narvik came on 28 May the Luftwaffe bombed the Allied ships providing naval gunfire support for the ground forces. In the fjord near Narvik the cruiser HMS *Cairo* was hit by a bomb and badly damaged. It was pulled out of the fight and sent to Britain for repairs. The next day, after Narvik had fallen to the Allies, the French cargo ship *St. Clair* was sunk by the Luftwaffe at Harstad.

German air operations were greatly reduced after 29 May by a spate of bad weather and only a few of the next ten days were flyable at all. This was a huge stroke of luck for the Allies, because in the first week of June all the Allied forces were evacuated without losses.

Allied air support at Narvik

The Royal Navy attempted to provide some air support for the Home Fleet squadrons operating in the Narvik area. But at the start of the campaign it had few resources. The carrier HMS *Furious* joined the Home Fleet on 10 April but carried only 18 Swordfish bombers, having left the ship's Skua fighters/dive bombers back at Scapa Flow. After an attack on German shipping at Bergen harbour that inflicted no damage, *Furious* moved to the Narvik area to support the Royal Navy and Allied ground forces concentrating there. On 12 April Swordfish attacked shipping in Narvik harbour, damaging some Norwegian merchant vessels the Germans had captured. The Swordfish supported the fleet attack the next day that destroyed all the remaining destroyers of the Kriegsmarine's Narvik group. The air support contributed little, and in two days of operations five Swordfish were lost to flak and operational accidents. On 18 April, *Furious* suffered propeller damage from a near miss from an He 111 bombing from high altitude, likely a German reconnaissance patrol. The *Furious* remained in the Narvik area for another week before returning to Scapa Flow, its Swordfish complement accomplishing little.

From the start of the campaign, the Allied forces had the use of a small Norwegian military airfield at Bardufoss, 80km north of Harstad. Bardufoss was a primitive airfield but was the home of a detachment of the old Fokker CV two-seater biplanes of the Norwegian Army Air Service, which provided reconnaissance and air support to the Norwegians during the April battles. Hundreds of local civilians were put to work at Bardufoss to clear the snow off the landing strip and build aircraft revetments to protect the aircraft from anything but a direct hit. The British attempted to put an airfield at Skånland near one of the Royal Navy anchorages by laying matting, but the ground at Skånland proved so wet that Bardufoss remained the only operable Allied airbase for the Narvik campaign.

On 21 May, RAF No. 263 Squadron, which had lost its aircraft at central Norway and then been re-equipped with 18 new Gladiators, arrived at Bardufoss. HMS *Furious* ferried the aircraft to 65km off Harstad. A Swordfish guided the Gladiators to their new airfield,

A Norwegian Fokker CV biplane light bomber/ reconnaissance plane, destroyed by the retreating Allied forces at Bardufoss in June 1940. A detachment of the Norwegian Fokkers provided air support to the Norwegian Army in its offensive against Dietl's troops at Narvik. (Author's collection)

Hawker Hurricane Mk I. RAF No. 46 Squadron, equipped with Hurricanes, was based for ten days at Bardufoss airfield near Narvik along with the Gladiators of No. 263 Squadron. The Hurricane, highly manoeuvrable with a top speed of 340mph, and armed with eight .303-calibre machine guns, was the most dangerous threat the Luftwaffe had to face in Norway. (© Hulton-Deutsch Collection/Corbis via Getty Images)

but the guide aircraft became lost in the overcast and flew itself, and two Gladiators following it, into a mountainside. All three aircraft were destroyed and only one pilot survived the crash. It was a memorable example of the daily dangers that pilots faced flying in Norwegian spring weather. Still, the Gladiators started flying immediately and challenging the German bombers.

On 26 May HMS *Glorious* ferried RAF No. 46 Squadron, equipped with 18 Hawker Hurricane Is, to Bardufoss. In fact, No. 46 Squadron had first attempted to land at Skånland airfield, which was south of the main Allied base at Harstad, but after three aircraft were damaged in landing accidents the squadron diverted to Bardufoss to be co-located with No. 263 Squadron. With two fighter squadrons at Bardufoss, the air battle over Narvik would be dramatically changed. The Allied naval and merchant ships now had some real defence from the German bombers, and, for the first time in the campaign, German air superiority was seriously challenged.

From 21 May to 7 June the two fighter squadrons were in action every day that conditions were flyable. Luckily for the Allies, the weather often intervened to prevent major Luftwaffe raids: of the last ten days of the campaign, 28 May to 7 June, weather permitted Luftwaffe attacks only on 28 and 29 May, and 2 and 7 June. On days that the weather was clear, RAF fighters had to fly constant patrols, as there was no early warning system to spot the Luftwaffe and the days were almost 24 hours long at those latitudes. Pilots would go for 48 hours without sleep. The logistics of the Bardufoss airfield were bare. Bardufoss was on a high plateau; as such, all parts, fuel and supplies had to be landed at the tiny port of Søreisa and brought up a steep and winding 27km-long track.

Despite the conditions, the two RAF squadrons accounted for more than 30 German aircraft over the Narvik area from 21 May to 7 June. They lost 16 of their own aircraft to combat and operational accidents during that time. The German bombers were at a disadvantage. With British fighters about, they needed Bf 110 escorts for any large raid, and the Bf 110s were flying long-range missions from Værnes and had only 20 minutes of fighting time over Narvik before they ran out of fuel.

The Luftwaffe lost more than 50 aircraft in missions to Narvik through May and June, most to fighters, but about 20 to Allied anti-aircraft and to operational accidents – the nemesis of flying in Norway, usually due to weather. While the attrition was wearing, Luftflotte 5 had reserve aircraft, and the air fleet's efficient logistics system ensured that replacement aircraft and aircrew could be passed up to Trondheim through Luftpark Oslo.

The final Allied attack on Narvik and evacuation

With Lt General Auchinleck's arrival, the final offensive against the Germans at Narvik began on 13 May when a strong French force, supported by heavy naval bombardment, landed at Bjerkvik, a town just 10km north of Narvik on the fjord. The town fell quickly, and Dietl's entire northern flank had to fall back to the shore of Rombaksfjord, almost to Narvik itself. Other French forces along with the Poles landed and advanced the Allied positions south of Narvik. Dietl's forces were now closely penned into their final defence line.

The decision of the Allied Supreme War Council to end the campaign in Norway on 24 May allowed Lieutenant General Auchinleck only a short time to take Narvik, destroy the port facilities to ensure the end of Swedish iron-ore shipments, and evacuate the Allied forces. The long-prepared attack on Narvik had been scheduled for the 21st but delayed to the 27th to have air cover from the RAF fighters that were just arriving at Bardufoss. The final attack would require an amphibious landing across Rombaksfjord by the French Foreign Legion brigade and a Norwegian battalion. On Narvik's southern flank, Polish battalions would advance against the defence positions of Dietl's improvised naval battalions. The Allies would have the advantage of artillery and naval gunfire support. Auchinleck began the attack in the evening of 27 May, although in that latitude it was still light. It was a textbook operation; as Allied warships poured direct fire into the German defence lines at close range, the French forces made the amphibious landings. In reply, Luftwaffe bombers from Trondheim had

Hurricane interception over Bardufoss, early morning, 7 June

To provide air cover for the Allied fleet at Harstad supporting the British/French/Norwegian ground campaign to take Narvik, on 26 May the RAF's No. 46 Squadron flew off the carrier *Glorious* for the small Norwegian airfield at Bardufoss, close to the Allied base at Harstad. The 18 Hurricanes reinforced the 18 Gladiator fighters of the re-equipped No. 263 Squadron that lost its aircraft in the debacle in central Norway in April. No. 263 Squadron had operated from Bardufoss since 21 May.

The raids by German bombers and Stukas, based at Værnes airfield at Trondheim, were the most serious threat to the Allied warships and transports supporting a ground force of more than 30,000 men. Conditions at Bardufoss were primitive, as the small dirt airstrip had few facilities to service aircraft. The German attackers and RAF defenders both had to contend with bad weather most days. On days with clear conditions, the Luftwaffe sent a series of bomber raids against the Allied base and shipping. With little darkness at these northern latitudes in late May and early June, the RAF Gladiators and Hurricanes had to fly constant patrol missions, and pilots often went 48 hours without sleep.

No. 46 Squadron, equipped with Hurricane Mk Is, inflicted a heavy toll on the German bombers, claiming 14 enemy aircraft between 27 May and 7 June, while losing three of their own number. Other aircraft were damaged in operational accidents or had suffered combat damage that could not be repaired. By 7 June both squadrons were whittled down to ten aircraft each.

This scene depicts one of the last aerial combats of the Narvik campaign, in the early hours of 7 June, when a flight of four He 111s from KG 26 appeared over Bardufoss from the northeast. The No. 46 Squadron commander, Squadron Leader Kenneth 'Bing' Cross, took off and was followed by his wingman, Pilot Officer Peter Lefevre. Climbing fast, the two Hurricanes approached the Heinkels as the German bombers turned south to evade the fighters. Cross selected the starboard Heinkel as his target and opened fire at close range and saw the right engine smoking. Cross broke off the combat when defensive fire from the Heinkel put 12 bullets into his plane that hit his windshield, engine and oil line, causing him to lose oil pressure. Cross managed to glide his aircraft back to a successful landing at Bardufoss. At first, Cross and Lefevre claimed the aircraft as a 'probable'. In fact, the Heinkel was so badly damaged by the British fighters it crashed near Narvik and the German aircrew were taken prisoner.

Luftwaffe bomber attacking a small merchant vessel in the North Sea, spring 1940. A large number of small naval trawlers and Norwegian coastal cargo vessels were employed by the Allies to transport troops, fuel and supplies to the small ports of Namsos, Molde, Åndalsnes, Bodø and Harstad during the campaign. More than two dozen naval trawlers and small merchant ships were sunk by German air attack in Norwegian waters. (Author's collection)

good weather the morning of 28 May and could attack Allied ships offshore Narvik. The British cruiser *Cairo* was hit by a bomb while it was supporting the Allied attack with naval gunfire. It was badly damaged and taken out of the battle. The German lines held just long enough to enable Dietl and his force to retreat from the city to a prepared defence line just short of the Swedish border. If pressed, he had the option of retreating to Sweden where his force would be interned – a defeat, but better than surrender to the Allies.

With Narvik taken on 28 May, the Allies finished demolishing the port facilities. Only on 1 June did the British and French governments tell the Norwegians that the Allied powers would evacuate all forces from Norway, and the evacuation was already under way as rear units began shipping out of Harstad. The Allied forces kept up the fiction that they were in Narvik to stay, while shipping convoys of troops and equipment back to Britain with escorts. Bad weather from 2 to 6 June kept German air reconnaissance from spotting the move. The weather cleared on 7 June and the RAF fighter squadrons, among the last units to evacuate, were still flying the morning of 7 June and managed to shoot down one He 111. As the British, French and Polish ground troops withdrew, the Norwegian 6th Division manned the line beyond Narvik, convincing the Germans that the vast Allied force was still there. The Norwegians held the line until the Allied evacuation, including that of their King and government, was complete. Then the remaining Norwegian military forces surrendered to the Germans on 10 June.

The last acts of the Norway campaign

Between 2 and 8 June 1940, Operation *Alphabet*, the evacuation of the Allied forces at Narvik, proceeded smoothly, aided by bad weather that prevented German flights for most days. HMS *Glorious* remained behind to provide air cover for the evacuation. Although No. 263 and No. 46 Squadrons were told to evacuate and destroy their aircraft, both stayed on with minimal ground crew to be ready to cover the evacuation. Indeed, on the morning of 7 June Hurricanes from No. 46 Squadron shot down a German bomber over Narvik. Both squadron commanders insisted on preserving their aircraft, certain they could land aboard *Glorious*, even though none of the pilots had ever landed on a carrier before. In a brilliant feat of airmanship, the ten remaining Gladiators from No. 263 Squadron and the ten remaining Hurricanes from No. 46 Squadron took off from Bardufoss and managed to land on *Glorious* without loss or mishap. The day after the last large convoys departed, HMS *Glorious*, escorted by two destroyers, left the Harstad area on 8 June.

In the meantime, the Kriegsmarine had developed its own operation, Operation *Juno*, as a means of helping the besieged German force at Narvik. The two remaining German battleships, *Scharnhorst* and *Gneisenau*, escorted by four destroyers, were ordered to proceed towards Narvik in hope of engaging the British fleet and supply convoys near Harstad. The same bad weather that had prevented German reconnaissance of the Allied evacuation allowed German surface forces to proceed undetected into the waters off western and northern Norway. Early on the 8th, the two German battleships came across a British merchant vessel and a tanker proceeding back to Britain, sinking both before they could sound an alarm. Proceeding to the waters off Narvik, the battleships spotted the funnel smoke from the *Glorious* and her destroyer escorts, HMS *Acosta* and HMS *Ardent*, at about 1545hrs. The *Glorious*, proceeding at the relatively low speed of 18 knots, had no combat air patrol flying, and neither did it have any aircraft ready for quick takeoff.

Moving at flank speed, the German battleships opened fire on the destroyer *Ardent* at 1627, at a range of 15km. The *Ardent* withdrew but was hit several times by *Scharnhorst*'s heavy guns and sank at 1725. After first firing at the *Ardent*, the *Scharnhorst* and *Gneisenau* quickly identified the *Glorious* and opened fire at 1632. The *Glorious* was struck in the third salvo of the *Scharnhorst*'s 283mm guns from a range of 24km. This first strike caused a large fire in the hangar that made it impossible for any aircraft to take off. Another salvo struck the bridge, killing the captain and most of the command staff. Further hits crippled the engine room. The *Ardent* and *Acosta* tried to lay a smokescreen and fired torpedoes at the *Scharnhorst*, one of which hit the battleship at 1730, causing heavy damage. As the *Glorious* was sinking, the German battleships turned their attention to the destroyers, sinking both with heavy guns. A total of 1,519 men died on the British ships. Only 40 men, including the commander of No. 46 Squadron, survived to be picked up two days later. The *Scharnhorst*, damaged and with heavy casualties, now needed to put into Trondheim for emergency repairs before returning to Germany. The *Gneisenau* returned directly to Germany.

The Fleet Air Arm was determined not to miss the opportunity to take out *Scharnhorst*. On 12 June, a Coastal Command reconnaissance plane spotted *Scharnhorst* at Trondheim's harbour. Fifteen Skuas of Nos. 800 and 803 Squadrons flying off the *Ark Royal* attempted to bomb *Scharnhorst* the next day, hoping to replicate the sinking of the cruiser *Königsberg* at Bergen on 10 April. But this time the Luftwaffe had a strong force at Værnes airfield, and German fighters intercepted the Skua dive bombers. Only a few of the 15 Skuas managed to drop bombs, and those missed. Eight Skuas were shot down by Trondheim's Bf 110 fighters and the survivors limped home to the *Ark Royal*, lucky to have survived the day. After temporary repairs, *Scharnhorst* left Trondheim and returned to Kiel to be repaired and refitted over the next weeks. This was truly the last action of the Norwegian campaign. The deficiencies of the Fleet Air Arm had been exposed, and the obsolete Skuas, having provided easy targets for the German air defence at Trondheim, were taken out of service and not used again.

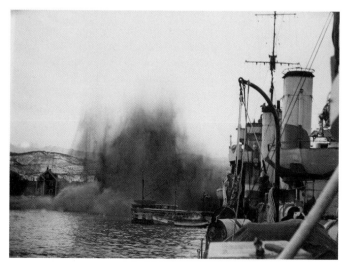

Luftwaffe bombing of Harstad late May 1940, the bomb exploding off the bow of the HMS *Ardent*. The Allies lost numerous ships sunk or damaged, mostly supply and cargo vessels, in the waters around Harstad and Narvik in May 1940. (Keystone-France/Gamma-Keystone via Getty Images)

ANALYSIS

The German campaign in Norway had ended victoriously. Ironically, the major motivation for intervention in Norway by both Britain and Germany – namely, the iron-ore shipments through the ice-free port of Narvik – had ceased to be relevant by the end of the campaign. In spring 1940, the Germans overran France and captured the vast iron-ore mines of Lorraine, which perfectly suited the German steel industry's needs, being much closer and easier for the transport of ore. Both the Allied and German destructions of the port of Narvik crippled it so badly that it was more than a year before the port could be used again for ore shipments. However, Germany gained some important strategic advantages from taking Norway. Its northern flank was now secure. Possession of Norway gave the Germans greater strategic reach out into the North Sea and across to the British Isles.

The Kriegsmarine's justification for seizing Norway – to base submarines at Trondheim – turned out to be irrelevant, like the iron-ore shipments. With the occupation of the French coast in June 1940, U-boats could be sent directly out into the North Atlantic from Saint-Nazaire and Brest, rather than Norway. Trondheim never became an important centre for naval operations, but the Germans still built a large submarine pen there. Though repeatedly bombed by Allied heavy bombers, its massive, concrete-reinforced structure proved impervious to Allied attacks. The submarine pen remains today, now used as a warehouse, the largest structure in the city of Trondheim.

In terms of casualties, the numbers came out fairly even. Some 4,000 German military personnel were killed. About the same number of Allied military personnel died. Naval losses were devastating for the Germans: at the start of the campaign they had the makings of a moderate-sized fleet; at its end, the surface navy was virtually out of action. Between April and June, the Kriegsmarine lost two cruisers sunk and two badly damaged; three battleships badly damaged; ten destroyers sunk, six damaged; and six U-boats lost. By summer 1940 the Kriegsmarine could send only a single squadron of cruisers and destroyers into battle.

For the Royal Navy and the Allies, the losses were as follows: one carrier lost; two cruisers sunk, three badly damaged; seven destroyers sunk, eight badly damaged; and four

British submarines sunk. The exiled Polish military lost one destroyer and one submarine, and the French lost a destroyer. Dozens of smaller vessels and merchant ships were sunk. However, unlike the Kriegsmarine, the Royal Navy could replace the losses. Aircraft losses were modest. The British lost 160 aircraft during the campaign; the Germans lost 242 aircraft, one-third of them transports.

Norway 1940 is important as the first modern joint warfare campaign in which all three military services – army, navy and air force – played essential roles. In Norway victory went to the side that could effectively coordinate ground, sea and air forces to achieve the objective. The Germans won because, in 1940, they understood joint warfare far better than their opponents and had practised it in training and actual combat. The British civilian and military leaders failed badly in 1940 because they had failed to understand how new aviation and communications technologies had radically changed warfare since World War I.

Crater from a Luftwaffe bomb in the port of Åndalsnes. Åndalsnes was heavily bombed several times by Luftflotte 5 bombers between 20 and 30 April. Despite the bombing, Sickleforce managed to evacuate by night without heavy losses. (Author's collection)

Air power was the key to victory in Norway 1940. The Germans used air power very effectively, while the British and Allied forces did not. The German planners made sure that decisive air superiority would be won on the first day and maintained through the campaign. Air superiority enabled the Germans to use their transport forces to move troops and equipment quickly to the strategic objectives. In the campaign, an impressive 29,000 troops were brought in by air transport, along with 2,000 tons of supplies and equipment. Air superiority allowed the Germans to provide extensive close air support and interdict the Allied logistics. The Germans also had an intelligence advantage, as their aircraft could freely roam over front lines and enemy rear areas to observe Allied dispositions and movement. In contrast, Allied ground forces in the battle for central Norway fought blind, with no ability to observe German dispositions or movement.

Important new methods of warfare were used in the Norway campaign with great effect: the use of paratroops and air-landing forces to seize strategic objectives, and air transport to quickly reinforce and supply forces isolated by sea and land forces. Both methods were essential to German planning and success. The use of paratroops and air transport should not have been such a surprise to the Allies. The Germans had already used air transport extensively in Spain and in Poland. The existence of the paratroops was no secret. Stories about use of Fallschirmjäger units to seize strategic targets during the Wehrmacht's annual manoeuvres were published in major magazines, and paratroops were openly discussed in military journals. Yet, the British military leaders were adamant that the superiority of the Royal Navy over Germany's small Kriegsmarine was so overwhelming that there was no possibility of the Germans invading Norway. The Royal Navy, in particular, saw naval warfare as a replay of the Battle of Jutland where numerical strength won a strategic victory. The Royal Navy's leaders were all veterans of Jutland and regarded battleships as still ruling the sea. Flawed assumptions usually lead to defeat in war, and British and Allied planning was based on a series of false assumptions.

Norway 1940 is unique as the first campaign which centred around airfields. The possession of airfields at Aalborg, Stavanger, Trondheim and Oslo determined the campaign – and it was airfields, not ports or ground armies, that became primary targets

General Erhard Milch (left), General Wolfram von Richthofen (right), taken June 1940. Milch was not liked by most of the Luftwaffe leaders owing to his closeness to the Nazi inner circle, and his love of intrigue and empire-building. But in Norway, he also showed himself to be a competent combat leader. (Author's collection)

of the RAF and Royal Navy. A few airfields gave the Luftwaffe the ability to control the North Sea, and for the first time in history naval power was overcome by air power. The Norwegian airfields gave the Luftwaffe the ability to reinforce the ground forces despite a tight submarine blockade.

Interestingly, the campaign in Norway was largely a naval air campaign, fought by two powers that had both neglected naval aviation before the war. The failure of the British to build a modern and effective carrier force was the fault of the Royal Navy, whose leaders preferred the battleship line, and the RAF, whose leaders focused on strategic bombing to the exclusion of other uses of air power. If Britain had had an effective carrier force, with better carriers and modern aircraft, they could have challenged German air superiority and provided Allied ground forces with air support. While the Luftwaffe failed before 1939 to appreciate the potential of naval aviation, the creation of X Fliegerkorps – a specialized anti-shipping bomber force – at the start of the war rectified some of the pre war failings.

Finally, the Norway campaign highlights the issues of leadership, planning and training. German operational leaders – von Falkenhorst, Milch, Geisler, Stumpff – performed very competently, responding to crises and making sound decisions quickly. In contrast, the top leadership of the British military – Ironside, Pound and Newall, and Forbes – developed a slow, bureaucratic decision-making process that failed to provide clear direction to the commanders on the ground. Interservice cooperation and planning in Britain was abysmal, and the campaign exposed major flaws in the British approach to joint operations. For their part, the German practice of co-locating operational army and Luftwaffe headquarters worked very well. The German operational planners from all services worked as a cohesive team and got the planning mostly right.

BIBLIOGRAPHY

Assmann, Kurt. *The German Campaign in Norway: Origin of the Plan, Execution of the Operation, and Measures against Allied Counter-Attack*. London: Purnell Books, 1974.

Bayer, James, and Ørvik, Nils. *The Scandinavian Flank as History: 1939–1940*. Kingston, ON: Queen's University Center for International Relations, 1984.

Boog, Horst. *Die deutsche Luftwaffenführung 1935–1945*. Stuttgart: Deutsche Verlags-Anstalt, 1982.

Byford, Alistair. 'False Start: The Enduring Air Power Lessons of the Royal Air Force's Campaign in Norway, April–June 1940', in *RAF Air Power Review* 13:3 (2010): 119–138.

Cameron, Ian. *Wings of the Morning: The British Fleet Air Arm in World War II*. New York: William Morrow and Company, 1962.

Claasen, Adam. *Hitler's Northern War*. Lawrence: University Press of Kansas, 2001.

Clemmesen, Michael and Faulkner, Marcus, eds. *Northern European Overture to War: 1939–1941*. Leiden, NL: Brill Academic Press, 2013.

Corum, James S. 'Stärken und Schwächen der Luftwaffe, Führungsqualitäten und Führung im Zweiten Weltkrieg', in *Die Wehrmacht: Mythos und Realität*, eds. Rolf-Dieter Müller and Hans-Erich Volkmann. Munich: R. Oldenbourg Verlag, 1999, 283–306.

Corum, James. 'Uncharted Waters: Information in the First Modern Joint Campaign – Norway 1940', in *Journal of Strategic Studies* 27:2 (2004): 345–369.

Corum, James. 'The German Campaign in Norway 1940 as a Joint Operation', in *Journal of Strategic Studies* 21:4 (1998): 50–77.

Crawford, Alex. *263 Squadron: Gladiators Over the Fjords*. Petersfield, Hampshire, UK: MMP Books, 2015.

Derry, T. K. *The Campaign in Norway*. Uckfield, UK: Naval & Military Press, 1952.

Derry, T. K., 'British Plans and Operations', in *Narvik 1940*, ed. Karl Rommetveit. Oslo: Institutt for Forsvarsstudier, 1991.

Dildy, Douglas. *Denmark and Norway 1940*. Oxford: Osprey Publishing, 2007.

Franks, Norman L. R. *Royal Air Force Fighter Command Losses of the Second World War*, vol. 1: 1939–1941. Leicester: Midland Publishing Limited, 1997.

Gemzel, Carl-Axel, *Organization, Conflict, Innovation: A Study of German Naval Strategic Planning, 1888–1940*. Lund, Sweden: Esselte Studium, 1973, 373–390.

Goulter, Christina. *A Forgotten Offensive: Royal Air Force Coastal Command's Anti-Shipping Campaign 1940–1945*. London: Frank Cass, 1995.

Haarr, Geirr. *The German Invasion of Norway, April 1940*. Barnsley, UK: Seaforth Publishing, 2009.

Hinsley, P. H. *British Intelligence in the Second World War*. New York: Cambridge University Press, 1979.

Hooten, E. R. *Phoenix Triumphant: The Rise and Rise of the Luftwaffe*. London: Arms and Armour Press, 1994.

Hubatsch, Walther. 'Weserübung'. *Die deutsche Besetzung von Dänemark und Norwegen 1940. Nach amtlichen Unterlagen*, 3rd ed. Göttingen, 1970. Google Scholar

Kersaudy, François. *Norway 1940*. London: Arrow Books, 1990.

Kiszely, John. *Anatomy of a Campaign: The British Fiasco in Norway, 1940*. Cambridge University Press, 2017.

Kühn, Volkmar. *Deutsche Fallschirmjäger im Zweiten Weltkrieg*. Stuttgart: Motorbuch Verlag, 1993.

Middlebrook, Martin and Everitt, Chris, eds. *The Bomber Command War Diaries: An Operational Reference Book 1939–1945*. Leicester, UK: Midland Publishing, 1996.

Militärgeschichtliches Forschungsamt, ed. *Kriegstagebuch der Seekriegsleitung 1939–1945*. Band 8. Herford: E. S. Mittler, 1989.

Moulton, J. M. *The Norwegian Campaign of 1940: A Study of Warfare in Three Dimensions*. London: Eyre & Spottiswoode, 1966.

Orange, Vincent. *Churchill and His Airmen*. London: Grub Street, 2012.

Ottmer, Hans-Martin. '*Weserübung': Der Deutsche Angriff auf Dänemark und Norwegen im April 1940*. Munich: R. Oldenbourg Verlag, 1994.

Ottmer, Hans-Martin. 'Das Unternehmen Weserübung: Die Besetzung Dänemarks und Norwegens durch die deutsche Wehrmacht im April 1940. Vorgeschichte, Vorbereitung und Durchführung der Landeunternehmungen in Norwegen', in *Ideen und Strategien 1940*, ed. Militärgeschichtlichen Forschungsamt. Herford: E. S. Mittler und Sohn, 1990.

Prien, Jochen et al. *Die Jagdfliegerverbande der Deutschen Luftwaffe 1934–1945, teil 3: Der Einsatz in Dänemark und Norwegen, 9.4. bis 30.11.1940 und der Feldzug im Westen, 10.5. bis 25.6.1940*. Eutin: Struve Druck Verlag, 2001.

Probert, Henry. *High Commanders of the Royal Air Force*. London: HMSO, 1991.

Richards, Denis, and Saunders, Hilary St. George. *The Royal Air Force, 1939–1945*, vol. 1. London: HMSO, 1953.

Rohde, Horst. *Das Deutsche Reich und der Zweite Weltkrieg, Band 2, Die Errichtung der Hegemonie auf dem europäischen Kontinent*. Stuttgart: Deutsche Verlags-Anstalt, 1979.

Roskill, S. W. *The War at Sea*, vol. I. London, 1954. Google Scholar

Schulze-Wegener, Guntram. 'Seestrategie und Marinerüstung', in *Die Wehrmacht: Mythos und Realität*, eds. Rolf-Dieter Müller and Hans-Erich Volkmann. Munich: R. Oldenbourg Verlag, 1999, 267–282.

Shores, Christopher. *Fledgling Eagles: The Complete Account of Air Operations During the Phony War and in the Norwegian Campaign, 1940*. London: Grub Street, 1991.

Taylor, Telford. *The March of Conquest: The German Victories in Western Europe, 1940*. Baltimore: Nautical and Aviation Publishing Company, 1991.

Vasco, John and Cornwell, Peter. *Zerstörer: The Messerschmitt 110 and its units in 1940*. Norfolk: JAC Publications, 1995.

Wegener, Wolfgang. *The Naval Strategy of the World War*, ed. and trans. H. Herwig. Annapolis, MD: US Naval Institute, 1989.

Ziemke, Earl. *The German Northern Theater of Operations: 1940–1945*. Washington: US GPO, 1959.